We cannot only hope to leave our children a bigger car, a bigger bank account. We must hope to give them a sense of what it means to be a loyal friend, a loving friend, a loving parent, a citizen who leaves his home, his neighborhood and town better than he found it.

George H. W. Bush

Design by Dietz Associates Inc., Kennebunk, Maine

www.kporttrust.org

ISBN 978-0-9774943-3-0

OUR PRESIDENT

loving memories of

GEORGE H.W. BUSH

FROM HIS FRIENDS IN THE KENNEBUNKS

Kennebunkport Conservation Trust, 57 Gravelly Brook Road, Kennebunkport, ME 04046

Mailing address: PO Box 7004, Cape Porpoise, ME 04014

207.967.3465   info@kctoffice.org

FOREWORD

He called Kennebunkport his "anchor to windward" and he loved it. He loved the ocean, whose surf broke against the rocky shore just below his bedroom window. He loved the smell of salt in the sea breeze and the way the moon rose over the lighthouse just up the coast. He loved the feeling of power in his speedboat *Fidelity* when he opened the throttle to skim across the waves and the gentle quiet in that same boat as he patiently cast his line in hopes of catching the perfect fish. He loved golfing at Cape Arundel, horseshoes by the house or a walk along the beach. He loved going downtown to stop into a store and say hello to a shop owner, going to dinner at Mabel's and feeling a part of a real Maine community. He loved his Walker's Point home and enjoyed sharing his blessing with others. In his youth he had been nicknamed "Have-Half" for his propensity toward sharing all that he had, and that trait never faded. The invitation list to his favorite place was legendary. World leaders, diplomats, actors, actresses, athletes, musicians, local businessmen, volunteers, friends, neighbors; all could find themselves being entertained at "The Point" and all could bear witness to the president's generosity and kindness. Indeed, there were times when even strangers were invited over. At the end of a speaking engagement or an interview

he might very well have said, "Why don't you join us?" and the staff would scramble to figure it all out. He loved his friends, and his loyalty to them would remain throughout his lifetime. It didn't matter whether he bonded with them in grade school, the Service, the grocery store or the White House, in George Bush you had a friend forever. Most of all, he loved his family, his wife Barbara, his children, grandchildren and great grandchildren. At Walker's Point he got to spend time with all of them, tighten the bonds of love that held them so closely together and draw strength from their closeness. He led a life of great challenges and great accomplishments, but with that came frequent change. Walker's Point in Kennebunkport was his constant, and even as he climbed to the highest office in the land, he never forgot his roots, his places of comfort or his friends—and we all loved him for it. More than that, we loved his incredible inclusiveness, his wonderful sense of humor, his willingness to help out a good cause, his faith and his commitment to serve. He was our president, but he was also our friend and neighbor. In that journey we shared together we were always left a bit better through his example. He generally also left us with a great story to tell, and on the pages that follow are some of them. Through these remembrances we hope that you will get to know him as we did.

Enjoy.

Tom Bradbury
Executive Director
Kennebunkport Conservation Trust

 CONTENTS

When two-term Vice President, then President, George H.W. Bush returned to Maine, the White House press followed; Bush was the story, and they were here to cover that story. If nothing else came from those twelve years of stories, Americans learned how to spell Kennebunkport.

When two-term Vice President, then President, George H.W. Bush returned to Maine, the White House press followed; Bush was the story, and they were here to cover that story. If nothing else came from those twelve years of stories, Americans learned how to spell Kennebunkport.

On his trips to Kennebunkport, President Bush, his family, staff, and the traveling White House press, would depart Andrews Air Force Base only to later land at Sanford Airport, 18 miles west of Kennebunkport. Here he greeted locals like Emile Roy—a barber and long-time friend. From Sanford, President Bush and his entourage zoomed toward Kennebunkport across the narrow rural roads the cops kept clear for him. The traveling White House press came later, arriving in Kennebunkport by bus.

Out back, behind the stately white-faced Colony Hotel, sat a squat red brick building that felt, at the time, like a storehouse for things unwanted. Here the hotel stored its broken lawnmowers, worn banquet tables and the White House press—it was our filing center.

The press shared the space with the folks from the White House Press Office. They produced printed transcripts of all official utterances (the world then free of Twitter and its tweets). Press Secretary Marlin Fitzwater held an occasional press conference or announced that we had a "lid on" meaning nothing newsworthy was expected and that sent reporters scurrying to the beach or a saloon.

Inside the filing center, there were wires everywhere, the longest of which snaked out of the building, up a little hill to a spot near the hotel pool where the television cameras lived. It made for an attractive location (with the hotel pool and ocean in the background) for TV reporters to do their stand-ups.

From the filing center, came a slew of predictable POTUS vacation stories, which frustrated the visiting Washington press corps who always wanted more. Apart from hints of war planning (that led to the 1991 Gulf War in Iraq), visits by French President François Mitterrand, Canadian Prime Minister Brian Mulroney, and U.K. Prime Minister John Major— who took hold of a live striped bass President Bush tossed to him (Major wriggled worse than the fish) not much hard news came out of Kennebunkport. What news there was (gobbled up by the local and regional broadcast media) included one or more of the following storylines: Bush goes fishing; Bush goes golfing; Bush goes to dinner; Bush goes to church.

Every now and again, there would appear a weighty long-form magazine piece crafted by some writer from away. They would opine on the economic impact of the Bushes on the town. They would ask if Kennebunkport was

9

10

LIFE IN A PRESIDENTIAL TOWN

to become the Republican Chappaquiddick? One writer I know took a tour of Dock Square. He peeked into every shop and restaurant—on the prowl for pictures of President Bush; he made a list of them and called them "Bush shrines" in his magazine piece.

Some came to Kennebunkport, not for the chance to see the President but instead to confront him. There were demonstrators opposed to abortion and others who arrived in town in support of a woman's right to choose. The unemployed demonstrated as did people who pressed to be heard on gun control or the environment. I remember one man in a worn black van who believed that President Bush was an extraterrestrial. And then there was the guy in the pink Tinker Bell costume who thrust his sequined wand towards Walkers Point declaring "Be gone, you have no power here."

After all the demonstrations in Kennebunkport in those years, I remember only one when the police appeared uneasy. Here is the headline that ran in the Los Angeles Times:

AIDS Protest Brings Issue to Bush's Door Demonstration: Beefed-up security in Kennebunkport assures distance between activists, President. Police guards wearing gloves are jeered.

"We wanted the demo to look like Cleopatra's entry into Rome, and be visible everywhere in town," said one of the organizers of the September 1991 demonstration by the AIDS Coalition to Unleash Power, or ACT UP. There were 1,500 demonstrators in town that day; there were no arrests.

That might have been the same Sunday when a group of forthright and earnest young people chained themselves to the doors outside the Kennebunkport post office. That's the sort of thing that can make the police a little itchy—but not Kennebunkport police chief Robert Sullivan. When I asked him why he withdrew his officers from the post office, he said, "Maybe they'll just leave." They did.

Lynn "Kip" Kippax

Lynn "Kip" Kippax lived in Kennebunkport for more than 20 years and reported on the goings-on at the summer White House for NPR and Maine Public Radio.

GOD BLESS AMERICA and GEORGE BUSH TOO!

13

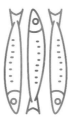

FRIENDS AND NEIGHBORS

On Wednesday, November 23, 1988, the first test of the new era was held. The Bushes arrived home and were going to speak on the River Green. All of the new players were in attendance. The national press corps was well represented. The local police force had been augmented by a large contingent of state troopers. The Kennebunk High School Band played Rudy Vallee's 'Maine Stein Song' in eager anticipation of the new first family's arrival. And the Secret Service had roped off the small River Green and asked all who arrived to pass through the town's first metal detector. State Representative H. Stedman Seavey took the microphone and addressed the crowd.

"During the course of this new administration, we as citizens of the Kennebunks should make this pledge to the president-elect," he stated as those assembled began to quiet down. "If he is willing to work to solve the problems of world peace, we in turn will work to solve the problems of traffic on Ocean Avenue. If he is willing to direct the world economy, we as a town can certainly direct a few tour buses. If he will pledge himself to uphold the moral character of government, we will pledge to maintain the rural character of Kennebunkport, his Maine home." The tone for the next four years had been set, the proper duties assigned.

FRIENDS & NEIGHBORS

17

A prolonged and enthusiastic ovation arose as President-elect Bush stepped to the front of the stage. He and Mrs. Bush scanned the faces of those nearby and waved an acknowledging hand of recognition to many. Then to his neighbors he said, "Thank you all, thank you, what a wonderful welcome back. Thank you for that very warm welcome.

"Just about eight-and-a-half years ago, you welcomed Barbara and me back right here in this exact spot; I was the vice presidential nominee of our party. And now you are welcoming back the next president of the United States of America. I'm very grateful to all of you. Barbara and I are glad to be back. And I hope you know how much we feel at home here.

"I'm 64, I hate to confess that, and I've spent at least part of 63 years of my life here. And I don't want to get too nostalgic, but this will date me. I used to bowl at the bowling alley, Bernie Warner's bowling alley, right across here, Harry Hamilton's.

"I'm trying to establish my credentials with some of you old timers. Mary Philbrick, I'm not talking about you, I have more respect for your age than that. But I knew the great Kennebunkport names when we were little. Clarks, Philbricks, Smiths, Etheridges, and I'm going to leave out too darn many—Reids and many others.

"And I remember being jealous—I was six. Booth Chick, I don't want to date him but he must have been ten or eleven. And he was racing up and down this river in a little skiff with a great big outboard motor on it. And I ate my heart out, and said someday I'd like to be able to do that.

"And my granddad, as you know, built that house out on Walker's Point about 1902 or 1903, and a couple of years before that my mother was born in a little house still standing out here on Ocean Avenue. And 22 years later or so she married my Dad in St. Ann's out on the coast there. Today we zoomed in there in a great big helicopter, and I wondered what my old man would say if he could see his little boy now.

"So what I want to say to you all . . . a lot of our roots are here. Part of what I really am is here. And I want Kennebunkport to retain its magic, and I want to come here a lot—that's not a threat. But I want to make some resolutions, some Thanksgiving resolutions.

"Nothing is going to interfere with the lobstermen who fish in that bay out there. They've been laying pots out there for many, many years and are going to keep on doing that.

"And I'll make this solemn pledge, I'm going to keep driving that fast boat, and when I get a line hung up on the propeller, I will do in the future what I've tried to do in the past; pick up the pot and find the guy that owns it and at least pay for the traps. So we'll keep doing that. And then I'll blame the Secret Service. But I promise to go slow in the river. I promise not to beat up on Sonny Hutchins or Ken Raynor at the Cape Arundel Golf Club.

19

"Barbara and I want to be good neighbors, and we're going to continue to—she is—to steal most of my books and give them to the little library up the street here (the Louis T. Graves Public Library, site of the old custom house). We're going to continue paying our taxes to Thelma Burrows' successor. In Kennebunkport, the town I love, we're going to continue to go downtown as we have—walk in or pop into the Book Port or to the Colonial Pharmacy or to Carl Bartlett's place at Port Hardware.

"We're not going to hold up traffic—well, we'll try not to hold up traffic," he laughed.

Then, the President-elect talked about those members of his transition team and Cabinet who had already tasted the hospitality of his Walker's Point home: Governor Sununu, Dick Darman, Nick Brady, Bob Teeter, Craig Fuller, and others.

"And because they've been here and seen our big family and all our friends here, they know why I love the place and they know I'm going to make them come back," he added. "And I'm going to do that regardless of what the problems are because everybody gets his strength from family, friends, and his faith. "I'm particularly concerned," he continued, "about the environmental problems facing the United States of America, especially every time I come to Kennebunkport and see the beauty of the ocean. And I do want to be the president to lead to the end of ocean dumping, to the preservation of our wetlands.

"Today I announced the appointment— some of you may have seen it—of a new national security advisor, a very distinguished American, a man who has served his country in the military and served his country in civilian pursuits in the White House. Today I named Lt. General, retired, Brent Scowcroft to be my national security advisor. And I think that is good for the United States. It will also help me to do something I feel very strongly about—work to enhance the peace, work to foster democracy and freedom around the world, work to fight for human rights.

"In closing let me say this. I have a wonderful feeling that the friendships we've made here in Kennebunkport will strengthen us, strengthen Barbara and strengthen me in the tough years ahead. The values I have learned here will help me through tough times. I want to say to all of you, my neighbors, I mean it when I say I don't want to complicate your lives, but I want to be a part of this community in the future as I have been for 63 out of the 64 years of my life. Thank you for this warm welcome. God bless you all. God bless this United States of America."

Tom Bradbury

Although my name is Annie Kennedy Phelps, everyone at the Point knows me as Annie the Gardener—even the President. In fact, I don't believe anybody there knew my formal name for years. I was sure "Kennedy" would not be a helpful name for employment there so I didn't test the waters. I found out that I could not be further from the truth. Everyone is welcome.

Just by the nature of my work, I had the great privilege of witnessing many private moments with the Bush family that represented how warm and down to earth they are.

Not too long ago, when President Bush was confined to a wheelchair, he came up to me while I was preparing the garden and volunteered to help plant the potatoes. There were obvious challenges but he overcame them in his own style. He decided to plant the spuds like a professional dart player. Concentrating so thoroughly that his lips formed into a circle, he aimed the spuds with accuracy into the trench I had prepared, flicking his wrist just so they would land in the right spot. It worked pretty well.

When I harvested them in the fall—he was excited. Holding a basket full of potatoes on his lap he headed on up to the Big House, saying as he was rolled away, "I wonder what Bar will think of these?" I didn't have the heart to tell him that she might not be too impressed as she had witnessed some of his more formidable accomplishments!

On another occasion, I had been working for his daughter Doro for a year when Mrs. Bush asked me to take over management of the rest of the gardens full time. It was fall and time to cut down all the perennial beds. Not knowing the layout of the house, I had no idea that the bedroom and private sitting area was right outside where I began clearing the gardens.

I was not aware that the president and Mrs. Bush were resting. As usual, I sang everything from gospel to Irish drinking songs the whole time. To my great horror, I found out that I was right under the open bedroom window during his "nap time". I later found out that he loved every minute of it; that began our singing relationship. Generally we would belt out a little tune when I saw him on his way to the office.

When he heard me singing or saw my blue hat he would ask the nurse to bring him closer. Sometimes I would pop out from behind a garden bed when he called my name and he would chime in to whatever tune I was singing.

After Mrs. Bush died and he returned to Walker's Point, there were a lot of people around. When I saw him, he asked me

22

how the place was shaping up. I told him I was trying to make sure it was the exact way Mrs. Bush would want it. He replied, "That is the way it should be, Annie." He knew your name, he knew your place in his life and he had respect for everyone.

The last time I saw him was the late summer of 2018 when he was being taken in his wheelchair to his office. Usually he was casually dressed in a golf shirt and a pair of khakis but this time he was dressed a little more formally with a crisp white long-sleeved shirt. I was filthy from digging in the gardens and stood there with a small planting shovel in my hand as his male nurse rolled his chair closer. When he was about 50 feet away I yelled "Hello there President Bush!" He smiled a broad smile of recognition. As he got closer I stuck out my elbow in greeting as I frequently did when covered in garden dirt. I did not want to get his shirt dirty. I commented on his more formal attire.

"Sir," I said, "you are all dressed up today. You must be about to greet someone important."

He looked at me and with a kind smile said, "Yes, Annie, and that would be you."

Annie Kennedy Phelps

I was truly humbled by a kind and great man who understood the value of respect for all.

"God Bless America" we sang, as God bless America we prayed.

Tom Bradbury

24

Bob Milne is our nation's foremost ragtime piano player, sharing his gifts and this classical art form in over 200 concerts a year. One of those concerts was scheduled immediately after the tragedy of 9/11, but he didn't know what to do.

Like all Americans, his heart ached over the senseless act of violence, sensing intuitively that the country he knew and loved would never be quite the same. What should his own personal response be, he wondered, as he walked the lonely streets of the city in which he had been set to play? Should he cancel the show, or should he stand up defiantly and echo the sentiments of his fellow countrymen who were joining as one to say, "We're here, we're proud and there's nothing that you can do to change that!"

"Play," his wife had encouraged him, "play."

"But what to play?" he asked himself over and over. Certainly it had to be something patriotic, but how would he choose? His wife had the answer for that question too. "Play them all," she said, and he did.

Bob told that story to a small group who had been invited by President and Mrs. Bush to hear him play their upright piano that had been turned slightly off the soft green living room wall so that the tiny audience might gain a better view of the artist. Drinks and appetizers had already been served, and the early fall sun was dipping lower over the small cove that separated their home from the mainland shore. President and Mrs. Bush were in the front row, with a diverse group of family, friends and neighbors behind. His story told, Bob sat down, put his hands on the piano's keys, paused for just a moment and then began to play

a song from the American Revolution. Over the next 40 minutes, one song wove seamlessly into another as he retraced the history and spirit of our union. Songs of the Civil War led to familiar melodies from World Wars I and II, and drew ever closer to the modern era. Then there was a moment of chaos before "New York, New York" was intertwined with the hauntingly beautiful naval hymn "Eternal Father Strong to Save", and all could instantly sense not just the enormity of our loss, but also the assurance that we would work through the challenges ahead and ultimately prevail. Next came the clear and well-known hymns from each branch of the armed services, one at a time, powerful and moving.

Unprompted, men and women who had served in those branches silently and reverently stood as their hymn was played, including President Bush whose eyes, like everyone else's in the room, glistened. The power and volume of the piano increased as the chords to "God Bless America" were belted out. By now, everyone was standing, emotionally singing, deep in their own thoughts and prayers. Tears were rolling down the President's cheeks, as they were for many.

"What could he be thinking?" we wondered, but the question had answered itself almost before the thought had been formed. He was thinking the thoughts of a patriot and father whose son now had the weight of the world on his shoulders, seen through the lens of perhaps the only person in the world who knew firsthand how heavy that weight could be. God Bless America we sang as God bless America we prayed.

Tom Bradbury

25

From left: President George H.W Bush, President George W. Bush, Austin's sister Carly, Austin's Mom Tammy Phillips, Austin, Austin's sister Ilyse and Mrs. Bush.

During one of my first summers working on Walker's Point, I quickly became involved in the Bush family dynamics. Mr. and Mrs. Bush made it a requirement that all summer lads were to come up to the Big House to eat lunch, which was prepped by their chef, Ariel. This is where I had my closest interactions with the family and their guests.

I will never forget three distinct moments during these lunch gatherings. First, when President Bush was fully healthy, he loved a good Bloody Mary or two or three. When he began taking medication, Mrs. Bush believed this was a bad idea and decided to cut him off. Barely a day later, President Bush came into the kitchen for lunch and asked Ariel to make him a Bull Shot. I laughingly asked him, "Sir, what in the world is a Bull Shot?"

"A drink that separates the men from the boys," he replied.

The next day, I helped Ariel make the same drink for the President. I had to look up the recipe. I then realized that our 41st President knew his mixed drinks well, favoring a more southern style, and nothing was going to stop him. I admired his perseverance.

Another time, President Bush invited famed golfer Phil Mickelson to come to the Point for a meal. When they were finished eating out on the deck, the President called my name. I came rushing, of course.

"Austin, I have someone I want you to meet," he said, as if it were someone just down the street. Sure enough, Phil Mickelson stood up and shook my hand. I was able to relate well with him because he too is a lefty golfer. President Bush said we were the odd ones in society. Mrs. Bush suggested that we all get in a picture together. This was one of the happiest moments in my life.

Finally, the day my father passed away, President Bush, who was now confined to a wheel chair, came down near the pool where I was working and handed me a note of condolence that he had written.

In his note he wrote that he had dealt with many deaths in his life, including the loss of his Mom, and it was the memories of those people and their lives which gave him the strength he had today. I was deeply touched.

The Bush family's impact has forever changed my life and I am forever thankful.

Austin Sandler

Austin with Phil Mickelsen

There are wooden ships, there are sailing ships, there are ships that sail the sea. But the best ships are friendships, and may they always be.

I don't keep a diary, but occasionally I write private notes after important personal or professional events. One occurred at Walker's Point in Kennebunkport on September 2, 2001. Mila and I had been spending our traditional Labor Day weekend with George and Barbara. And towards the end, he and I had a long private conversation. My notes capture the moment.

I told George how I thought his mood had shifted over the last eight years, from a series of frustrations and moments of despondency in 1993 to the high enthusiasm that I felt at the Houston launch of the Presidential Library and George W's election as governor in November of that year, to the delight following Jeb's election in 1998, followed by their great pride and pleasure with George W's election to the presidency and, perhaps most importantly, to the serenity we found today in both Barbara and George. They are truly at peace with themselves, joyous in what they and the children have achieved, gratified by the goodness that God has bestowed upon them all and genuinely content with the thrill and promise of each passing day.

And at that, George, with tears in his eyes as I spoke, said, "You know, Brian, you've got us pegged just right and the rollercoaster of emotions we've experienced since 1992. Come with me."

He led me down the porch at Walker's Point to the side of the house that fronts the ocean and pointed to a small, simple plaque that had been unobtrusively installed just days earlier. It read C-A-V-U. George said, "Brian, this stands for ceiling and visibility unlimited. When I was

a terrified 18 to 19-year-old pilot in the Pacific, those were the words we hoped to hear before takeoff. It meant perfect flying. And that's the way I feel about our life today, C-A-V-U. Everything is perfect. Bar and I could not have asked for better lives. We are truly happy and truly at peace."

As I looked over the waters of Walker's Point on that golden September afternoon in Maine, I was reminded of the lines, simple and true, that speak to the real nature of George Bush and his love of his wonderful family and precious surroundings.

Brian Mulroney
Former Canadian Prime Minister
Remarks made in the State Funeral for
President George Herbert Walker Bush

He was a fine leader—
and a wonderful man.

This is a letter— about a letter—about a letter.

Our family has had a summer home on Hoyt Neck in Biddeford for many years. We love to boat and, in fact, we have parked our boat *Unplugged* near President's Bush's *Fidelity* at the Kennebunkport Marina for many years. Fishing is always a happy, precious family time.

Over the years we had a few short boat-to-boat fishing intel exchanges with President Bush at different fishing spots along the coast—at the mouth of the Saco River, around Cape Porpoise, sometimes right off our rocks at Hoyt Neck. This was always very exciting for us, especially as the Secret Service flotilla arrived—always in hot pursuit of a full throttle *Fidelity*!

One day back in 2001, my then eight year-old son, Andrew, his friend Tommy LaPorte and I were fishing off Hoyt Neck. Suddenly, *Fidelity* came into view moving at a high rate of speed. We were amazed when the President executed a VERY high speed u-turn, then pulled in "to see how we were doing." At that point we had no bites—but Andrew reported what baits and lures we had tried so far. President Bush wished us well and headed off.

As luck would have it, just a few minutes later, Andrew hooked a large striper—the biggest he ever had on a line. Andrew reeled frantically while Dad held him around the waist so he wouldn't get pulled in. He successfully landed the fish, Tommy took a quick photo, and we let it go, "so it would get bigger."

When we got home, Andrew shared the exciting news about the monster fish and our visit from the President.

The next morning Andrew felt strongly that we should write President Bush a letter because "we need to tell him about the bait we used so he can catch one too." So the two of us carefully penned a letter explaining our fishing good fortune and advising the bait we had used. We did not expect a response.

A few weeks later we were thrilled to receive a very kind response. That personal letter will always be treasured. It is framed and on our wall at the house.

We write this letter—about a letter— about a letter—to share our little story (among thousands of others we are certain) of President Bush's small but important impact on our family.

But it's also a story of just another guy with a love of boating, fishing, and our spectacular Maine coastline. He was a fine leader—and a wonderful man.

The Tolley family

31

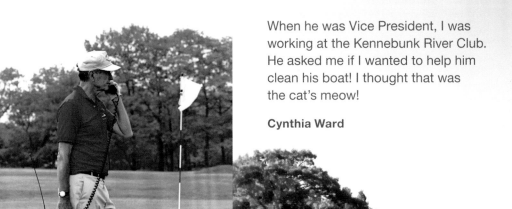

When he was Vice President, I was working at the Kennebunk River Club. He asked me if I wanted to help him clean his boat! I thought that was the cat's meow!

Cynthia Ward

In 2003, my wife Nancy and I were invited to have dinner with Barbara and George Bush at Walker's Point. We were instructed to dress casually and bring our putters. The President had just installed a new putting green next to his home and wanted his guests to try their skill. We arrived with about 15 other guests and were delighted to find that Phil Mickelson, the famous professional golfer, and his wife Amy were staying with the Bushes. Everyone, including Phil, participated in an informal putting contest, which Phil won by defeating Nancy in the finals. It was a wonderful evening with many golf stories shared. I am not sure whether the new putting green improved the President's putting but, as in everything he did, he never stopped trying to do things better!

Dick Thigpen

In the early 2000s I was president of Cape Arundel Golf Club. One summer day, in my first year serving in that position, I was walking out of the clubhouse when I heard from across the parking lot, "Hey, Mr. President. How are things?" I looked up and saw President Bush smiling at me. "Fine, Mr. President", I replied, "Just fine." Same title, I thought, but a bit of difference in responsibility.

George Bush – a great man with a common touch.

Bill Matthews

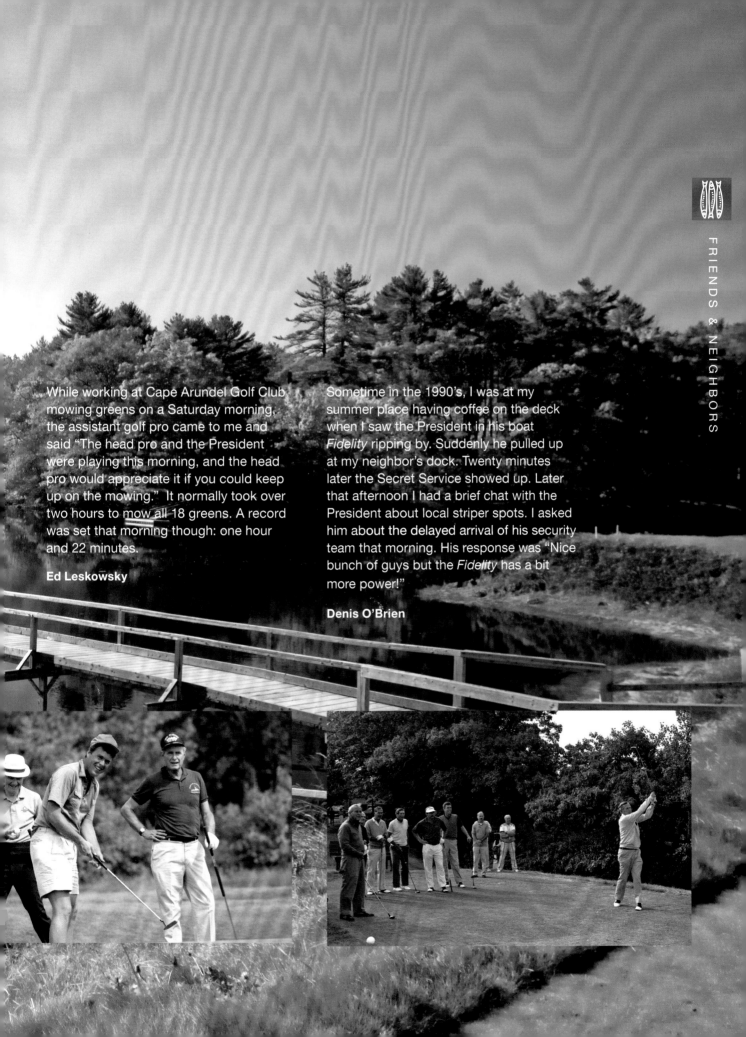

While working at Cape Arundel Golf Club, mowing greens on a Saturday morning, the assistant golf pro came to me and said "The head pro and the President were playing this morning, and the head pro would appreciate it if you could keep up on the mowing." It normally took over two hours to mow all 18 greens. A record was set that morning though: one hour and 22 minutes.

Ed Leskowsky

Sometime in the 1990's, I was at my summer place having coffee on the deck when I saw the President in his boat *Fidelity* ripping by. Suddenly he pulled up at my neighbor's dock. Twenty minutes later the Secret Service showed up. Later that afternoon I had a brief chat with the President about local striper spots. I asked him about the delayed arrival of his security team that morning. His response was "Nice bunch of guys but the *Fidelity* has a bit more power!"

Denis O'Brien

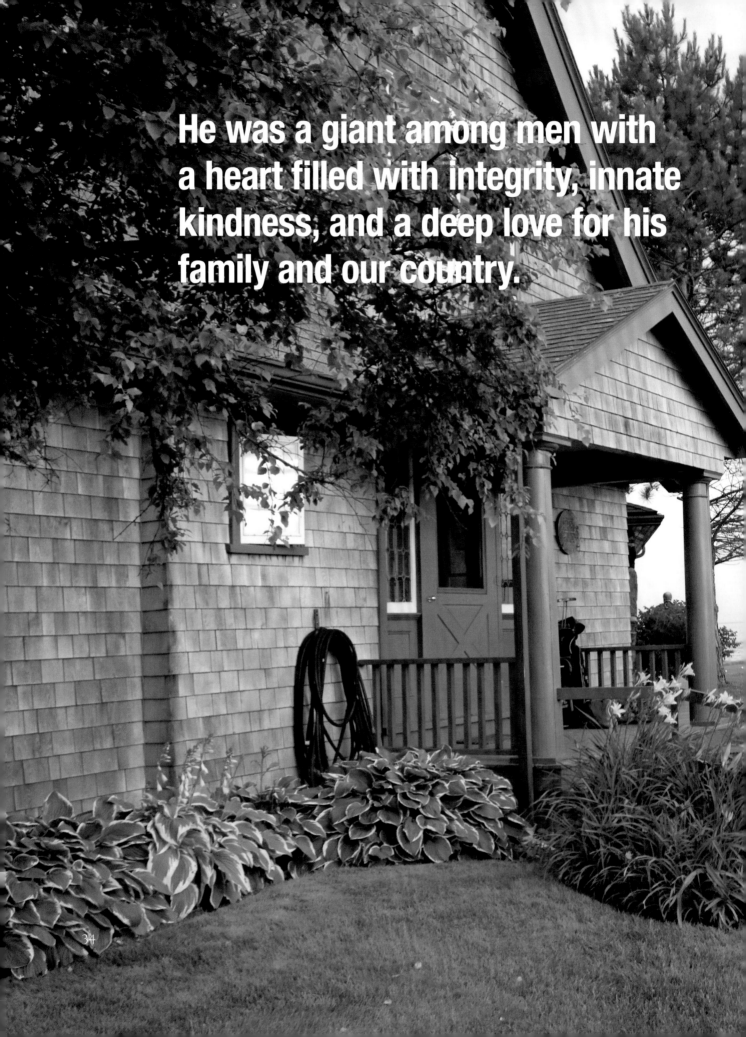

He was a giant among men with a heart filled with integrity, innate kindness, and a deep love for his family and our country.

34

I had the honor and privilege of landscaping and maintaining the property at Walker's Point for many years. During that time I had the wonderful opportunity to know President Bush quite well. I experienced early on his very caring nature.

It was usual for him to stop and chat while I was working. He often asked about my family. One time he asked me to ride to Walmart with him. On another morning he introduced me to President Bill Clinton as they were leaving to play golf. On some summer days he insisted I take a break and join him by the pool to chat over freshly baked cookies.

While in Houston for the winter, sometimes he would call. "Good morning, Doug," he would say. "Barbara and I are sitting drinking our coffee and thought we'd call to see how your winter is going."

Then there was the time he pointed out his favorite tree on the property, which was slowly being destroyed by vines and overgrowth. He sincerely seemed concerned and wanted me to try to bring it back to flourishing health. A month or so later, Mrs. Bush took me to the same tree, pointed at it and said, "This is George's favorite tree, but I hate it and I want you to cut it down over the winter while we're gone. And, oh, Doug," she added, "don't tell anyone about it. This will be our little secret. He'll never notice it's gone." It was an interesting situation, to say the least. Fortunately, I was able to work it out by following Mrs. Bush's advice so that both were happy.

My wife and I will always cherish the special events we were invited to attend, including the commissioning of the new aircraft carrier bearing his name, his 90th birthday party, the celebration of the 100th anniversary of Walker's Point and many more.

He was a giant among men with a heart filled with integrity, innate kindness, and a deep love for his family and our country.

Doug Coleman

This is a book about reflections, and when I look back at my life of bountiful blessings I can clearly see the certain Hand of God. For example, I am told I almost died at childbirth, but somehow survived. I also had (to me) the most amazing parents, each of whom taught me about service in their own unique and penetrating ways. Then there are my incredible wife, my mostly wonderful kids, and loyal friends.

But there can be no question that knowing, helping and serving George and Barbara Bush was by far the greatest and surest sign that the good Lord had put me on this earth to do more than merely mark time. And if you knew George and Barbara Bush, one of the greatest benefits—aside from their many adventures, and their innate decency—could be time spent in Kennebunkport.

The President's 90th birthday in Maine stands out as a powerful memory. A month or two before the date, our beloved 41 had decided he wanted to make what would prove to be his final parachute jump. When I heard this, I was dumbfounded as, by then, vascular Parkinsonism had robbed his legs of his ability to stand. Yet, I was told the highly-skilled ex-Army experts with whom the President would be jumping had a plan to make everything work. I remained unsure.

As the date approached, I also had a special challenge as the President's spokesman. The ever-intrepid Associated Press reporter David Sharp kept asking if there were special plans for the big date. David, I am sure, was well aware of the President's penchant for parachute jumping every five years to mark his 75th, 80th and 85th birthdays. By then, David also knew that 41's deteriorating mobility meant, to most mortals at least, that his ability to jump was non-existent. But David was not sure, and pro that he is kept probing me about it.

Is there any doubt that George Herbert Walker Bush is the greatest man any of us will ever know, and not just because he was President?

37

At the age of 90—and being at the mercy of the coastal Maine weather patterns—we wanted to preserve the President's ability to back out if such a jump was not in the cards without disappointing too many people. So I had to be vague when responding to David's direct inquiries about birthday plans. I cannot recall exactly how I ducked and dodged, but it was tricky. And my side of the story is I never misled David, though I might not want to testify to that under oath.

June 12, 2014 dawned foggy and not exactly balmy. This was not "Ceiling and Visibility Unlimited." But the question was: Where would the cloud ceiling be, and could the helicopter get up high enough—and safely enough—to permit a proper jump? It was touch-and-go for an hour or two. Wondering along with us was Jenna Bush Hager, 41's granddaughter, and her NBC crew who were there to capture the entire escapade from start to (hopefully) happy finish.

Have you ever met a kinder, more understanding, more decent, and more accomplished person in your life?

FRIENDS & NEIGHBORS

39

Lech Wałęsa

Gdańsk, 12 June 2014

His Excellency George H.W.Bush
41ᵗ President of the United States of America

Dear Mr. President, Dear Friend,

On this very special day I wish you happy birthday, all the best in good health and strength to achieve more and more for your country and all of us, who are congratulating you on this splendid occasion. Let me also express my deepest gratitude to you for your public service and great activism in so many fields you have been committed to.

Your wise and courageous leadership, rooted in dialogue and responsibility, led to a peaceful shift of forces in the world. Although living far away, you have always been close to us, to Poles. You did not forget about Poland in the hard period of international turbulences and fundamental transformation in the 1980s. While celebrating 25 years of the democratic transition in my country, we do remember your personal contribution to that challenging political breakthrough. Better than anyone, you could understand the true difficulties we were going to face while entering the new way of freedom. When back in 1989, during your visit to Gdansk, you spoke with admiration of Solidarity, we were certain that the lofty wording would be followed by specific declarations and decisions, which did take place. Had it not been for solidarity – international solidarity and American solidarity, we would not have won freedom!

I also cherish the recollections of the many meetings we held, as well as of the warm and friendly welcome I received from Barbara and you when you hosted me both in the White House and in your unique Maine and Texas homes. I am hopeful that despite the distance between Gdansk and Houston we will have an opportunity to meet again, recall the past, yet also share our insights into today's world and the challenges it faces.

May you long continue enjoying wonderful moments amidst your loved ones and friends who have so much respect for and gratitude to you.

Faithfully yours,

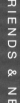

Finally, we got word that the weather would cooperate just enough so the jump could go on. That's when we announced to the world, via the President's Twitter feed, that "It's a wonderful day in Maine—in fact, nice enough for a parachute jump." The surprise had held and, as 41 had no doubt intended, wonder was in the air.

Coordinating coverage with Jenna and her crew meant I was there when the 41st President arrived at the helicopter launch area near the staff office on Walker's Point. I greeted him just before he boarded, and the man I saw that morning was as serene, fulfilled, and joyful as I had ever seen him. After take off, I moved over to St. Ann's church grounds—the designated landing zone—to help the camera crew capture the landing.

I feel, like so many of you, that seeing that great and good man floating earthward in the splendor of the Maine sky after the chute opened, probably giving him a look at his beloved seacoast not unlike the one he and his devoted bride enjoy today, was pure joy. The landing, in which the President's tandem partner Mike Elliott attempted to land horizontally with the President dragging his legs behind him, was not the smoothest—but he gave a quick thumbs up to assure us all was well.

The sight of George Bush kissing his amazing wife, shaking the hand of the 43rd President, and basking in the joy and admiration of four generations of his family and so many Maine friends will remain with us all forever.

Is there any doubt that George Herbert Walker Bush is the greatest man any of us will ever know, and not just because he was President? Have you ever met a kinder, more understanding, more decent, and more accomplished person in your life?

Further testimony comes from this letter George H. W. Bush received that same day, his 90th birthday, from former Polish President Lech Walesa—the charismatic union electrician who bore true witness to the liberation of Poland and Eastern Europe during the 1980s and 1990s. President Walesa's words offer a powerful reminder of George Herbert Walker Bush's remarkable impact on our world, and those of us fortunate to be among his legion of friends.

Jim McGrath
Spokesman, Office of George H. W. Bush (1993-2018)

41

Our family met President Bush in August of 1989. Our father, Ron Goyette, presented the First Family with a painting of Walker's Point at a ceremony where President Bush was honored as "Man of the Year" by the Kennebunkport Chamber of Commerce.

Dad was an artist who moved to Kennebunkport in 1970 and specialized in turn of the century scenes and seascapes. He founded the Art Guild of the Kennebunks and was vice president of the Kennebunkport Chamber of Commerce in the 1980s.

Dad was honored when the Chamber asked him to paint for the First Family. He enjoyed researching their Maine home for the project. He was excited to both create the painting and to present the Bushes with this unique gift. The ceremony was held outside on a hot, windy day in August. During the presentation, the painting started to tip on the easel. Our father quickly pointed to the painting, afraid it would fall, and liked to tell the tale that several Secret Service agents responded to his gesture by reaching into their coats, ready to handle any potential threat.

The painting now resides at the George H.W. Bush Presidential Library and Museum in Texas where visitors can enjoy it as much as President Bush once did.

The Goyette children

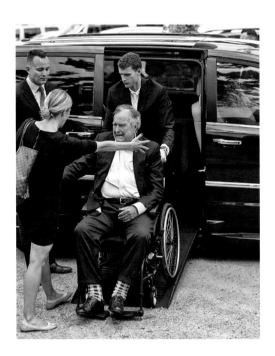

I had the privilege of working with President George H.W. Bush from 2000 and throughout the remainder of his remarkable life. Usually I was the person behind the scenes. Yet, every event started the same: the President always greeted me with a boisterous "Brookie!" and a big hug and kiss. He was so kind, caring and genuine. I have so many stories and memories to treasure of this inspiring man and his family.

Brooke Sheldon

When President Bush was Vice President, our friends Dan and Mary Philbrick went to Florida with my husband Sandy and me. Vice President Bush, whom we knew personally, invited us to stop off in DC. It so happened that when we got there he was called upon to leave for China on a mission. He was kind enough to leave us a car and his driver who for the next two days took us wherever we wanted to go. The driver, a Master Sergeant in the Air Force, treated us like royalty per orders from the Vice President. One morning, just before going to breakfast at the hotel, we told the desk clerk that we would be in the dining room and asked if he would please let us know when the Vice President's car came for us. His smug remark was "Sure I will." About half an hour later he entered the dining room with a very professionally delivered announcement that our car had arrived.

Carol MacKinnon

When I graduated from Kennebunk High School in 1987, Bush 41 was the Vice President of the United States. He was at our graduation and he personally handed out all the diplomas to my graduating class, shook each graduate's hand and congratulated each of us personally. This was the first of many positive interactions I have been honored to have with him over the years.

Shelley Wigglesworth

While attending college in 2003 I was also working at the Biddeford Home Depot to help our young family make ends meet. One day President and Mrs. Bush came to the store accompanied by several Secret Service agents. They just walked the aisles chatting with everyone. At one point, there were about ten of us around him answering questions in the hardware tool corral. Mrs. Bush leaned over, put her hand on my shoulder and whispered, "George just loves tools." It was very sweet and very human.

David Bowen

After we established the York County Elder Abuse Task Force, President Bush helped us to pull off an amazing Wishing Well Wish for a very special Maine senior citizen. Millie Remmie had always wanted to meet him. When we made the request, he graciously agreed and the meeting was a memorable one for all.

Candice Simeoni

It was a beautiful September day in the Kennebunks and the town Republicans were all fired up. My wife Nancy and I, having just returned from the National Republican Convention as delegates for George H.W. Bush, were really excited. We were on hand to open a local Bush for President headquarters in two hours.

We secured a great location at the corner of Christensen Lane and Route 35 in Kennebunk's Lower Village, which is just across the Kennebunk River from Kennebunkport. Now the office space had to look like a presidential headquarters. Television reporters and other news media were due to arrive and, yes, we needed their publicity.

Our impressive two by twenty foot Bush/Quayle exterior banner was waiting to be hung. Bless the rugged guys with tall ladders and the courage to do the job—it looked awesome.

As for the inside, a variety of donated desks, tables, chairs, and lamps, stood by; but how to arrange a mismatched collection of furniture and make it look good? Gifts from the heart don't necessarily conform.

Debbie Reid and volunteers took on the job, turning twentieth century attic into a welcoming and efficient VIP campaign headquarters. Wall hangings? No problem! We would include not only Bush/Quayle information but political signs of local GOP candidates: John McKernan for Governor, Olympia Snowe for Senate, David Emery for Congress, Tom Murphy and Stedman Seavey for the Maine house, and Wes Phinney for Sheriff. The assortment of signs with varied colors and designs made everything look great. Bingo! Headquarters ready, mission accomplished.

With time getting short and excitement growing, I stepped outside to view the finished product. As I looked down the driveway I suddenly noticed Mrs. Dorothy Walker Bush, the President's mother, approaching. Oh no, a moment of panic—I'd overlooked inviting her to the opening of the headquarters. Immediately I greeted her and apologized that I had neglected to call her. A very gracious woman, she assured me it was not a problem; she was eager to see what had been made ready for her son's campaign.

My oversight never happened again. Throughout many years of numerous Bush events, I always made sure there was a call and invitation to Walker's Point for the President's mother. Of all the visitors we welcomed during that time, Dorothy Walker Bush was my favorite. She was truly a lovely, genuine lady. It was clear who had raised the President.

John Downing

During the summer of 2008 I started walking with President Bush a couple times a week. We usually followed a route that took us through the nearby Kenneth Roberts Estate, which was located across Ocean Avenue a short distance from Walker's Point. We would walk all the way to the end, sit on the stone wall and rest before turning around and going back; we were usually trailed by one Secret Service agent on foot and a couple more driving slowly in an SUV.

Our routine involved telling silly jokes like " How many balls of string does it take to go from the Earth to the moon?" The answer is "One, if it's long enough."

As many people know, he loved to grade jokes. He never gave me a good grade. NEVER. I always complained about my poor grades and he would always tell me not to whine. Our routine also involved picking up trash. President Bush would point to a wrapper or a bottle with his walking stick and I would scoop it up. Our walks always included a bit of spirited baseball talk. He loved the Astros and referred to me as a rabid Red Sox fan. Sometimes he reminisced about his days playing first base at Yale.

I regret that I did not keep a journal of this time. I thought I would remember everything, but of course I do not. One incident does stick out though. It was our last walk of the season

before the Bush's headed back to Houston the next day. President Bush pointed to a house as we walked by and proudly said, "They know me." He explained that when he was President and wanted to go for a jog, he often had to run down a private road alongside the house. He said the owners never complained.

Apparently feeling inspired, he suddenly said "Let's go say hi!" We walked up to the door and rang the bell. I knew someone was home because the TV was blaring. I will never forget the look on the face of the older woman when she saw President Bush smiling at her through her front door. She could barely speak.

"Come on in," she said, recovering her wits. We followed her to the living room where her husband was seated in front of the TV watching CNN at full volume. He did a double take when he saw the President. I think they were too stunned to think clearly as they never thought of turning down the TV. I cannot say for sure that anyone could hear anything but we stayed about 10 minutes. When we said goodbye, little did they know there was still another surprise to come.

The next day I received an email from President Bush who was already on his way to the airport. He asked me if I could stop by his office where he had left a bottle of champagne and a letter on his desk. He asked if

President Bush was hands down the most fun and thoughtful friend ever.

I would please take those items to the nice couple we had visited the previous afternoon. I was thrilled to be able to do a favor for President Bush so I jumped on the opportunity. Unfortunately no one was home when I arrived so I did not get to see their reaction. I left the goodies in the mailbox. To this day I love to imagine their surprise when they opened the mailbox.

President Bush was hands down the most fun and thoughtful friend ever.

Nancy Sosa

49

Many years ago I went to the Memorial Day Parade in Kennebunkport. I had heard that President Bush liked massages so I put a business card in my back pocket and after his speech made my way up to him, put my hand out to shake his hand, and said "Mr. President, it's so nice to finally meet you and I hear that you like massages. If you'd ever like a great massage, here's my business card." He stopped and chatted with me and I got a photo taken with him. He called me the following week and I have been providing massages to him, Mrs. Bush and the rest of the family ever since.

Pamela Cummings

51

On a crisp, late September morning in 2009, Ocean Avenue, at a point near where it passed by Walker's Point, was closed to traffic for a few hours so friends could surprise President Bush by unveiling the Anchor to Windward monument in his honor. Around a hundred guests, many of them ringing cowbells, sat in folded seats which had been set up right in the middle of the street, facing the tarp-covered anchor. A bagpiper stood on the rocks in the distance, playing Anchors Aweigh as Blowing Cave spewed the crashing waves skyward. The scene was perfectly set for President Bush's arrival.

President Bush thought he was going to Cape Arundel to visit his close friend Ken Raynor when his SUV came to a sudden halt just a few yards after exiting Walker's Point. Tom Bradbury, the executive director of the Kennebunkport Conservation Trust, the organization that had planned the event and the anchor placement, and

I were there to greet him as he got out of the car. As the President exited the car, he said, "What the hell is going on?" We said nothing. "Seriously, what is going on?" he asked again.

President Bush placed his hand on my shoulder for balance as we approached the cheering crowd. Once President Bush took a seat next to Bar, their dog Bibi at his feet, the ceremony began. Friends and neighbors took turns sharing heartfelt stories until it was time to unveil the three-ton Navy anchor. President Bush truly seemed surprised and touched by the festivities, so much so that he invited everyone over to Walker's Point on the spot. He wanted everyone to see why he loved Walker's Point. No surprise that everyone took him up on his kind invitation.

It was the happiest of days, which I will remember forever.

Nancy Sosa

I've known George and Barbara since the 1960's. They are the nicest people you could ever meet. My dad and mother were great friends with both of them for many years. While driving my parents to a Florida inn the 1980s, we stopped in DC and got a VIP tour of the White House and a White House car to drive us around. They were very nice people and down to earth. Once while visiting, I took a picture of Barbara in her nightgown with their dog Millie and she jokingly warned me never to show that to anyone or I would be in trouble! My family has many photos of the Bushes but my most prized picture is with my parents, my big brother Dan and myself in the Oval Office.

Peter Philbrick Sr.

54

Working at Walker's Point and serving President George H.W. Bush and Barbara has been a highlight of my catering career and my life. It was an honor to be working in their home. My crew came to know and love the Bushes as much as I do.

Over the past 13 years, the Kitchen Chicks team has catered to Bush family members for weddings, baptisms, birthdays, Sunday dinners and even luncheons by the pool. We have also been on the Point for many fundraising events with senators, former ambassadors and Bush cabinet members, PGA Golf pros, acclaimed authors and members of the press. Interesting and important people, yes, but the first thing made very clear at the Big House on Walker's Point was that the Bush dogs rule in the family hierarchy. Never feed them, but do expect them to be under foot at any time so watch out and make way!

Bibi and Minnie along with Doro's dogs were happily part of every celebration. And later when Sully the service dog arrived, we were smitten with the handsome, talented canine.

It's not actually work when you enjoy your time with this family as much as we did. Arriving and unloading extra early, polished and prepped within an inch of our lives, we would relax as soon as President Bush came through the kitchen and exclaimed in a loud voice, "The Chicks are here!" He would greet us all and later offer thanks and a compliment on his favorite bacon wrapped hors d'oeuvre. One time as he was wheeled past the kitchen President Bush yelled out, "It was great Peggy. I pigged out!" Best compliment ever!

Each year, when they returned to Walker's Point, the summer retreat they so loved, their happy anticipation of another joyous season on the coast of Maine was infectious. At our last event each fall, before 41 and Mrs. Bush flew back to Texas, I would start to feel a sense of angst and worry. Would they be back next year? Would their health hold out? God willing, we would have more time with them for another summer in Kennebunkport.

I have so many fond memories of President and Mrs. Bush and their amazing family. I am beyond grateful.

Peggy Liversidge

My parents and I were blessed to attend many special events and gatherings over the years thanks to the benevolence of President and Mrs. Bush. One of my favorite memories took place when I was a college student majoring in art history. At the time I was an intern at our local Brick Store Museum and helped to curate an exhibition on Walker's Point called *An Anchor to Windward: The Maine Connection*. The exhibition was sent to Texas where it was displayed at the George H. W. Bush Presidential Library and Museum in College Station from March 6, 1999 through August 9, 1999.

The Brick Store Museum organized a group of about 120 Bush family friends and neighbors to travel to Texas for the grand opening of the exhibit, my parents and I included.

The group toured the Bush Library and Museum on our first morning there. The museum was impressive and I remember being struck by how many references there were to the "Summer White House" throughout the permanent exhibit.

Clearly Kennebunkport held a special place in the president's heart. Later that day while the group was enjoying lunch at a Texas ranch, my dad was helping to set up a traditional Maine lobster bake provided by Ed and Sheila Bull whose custom-made t-shirts depicting lobsters traveling from Maine to Texas were a big hit! President Bush dropped by twice

that afternoon to personally check on the preparations. The lobster bake took place after entertainment by the Texas A & M Country Dance Team, and my parents were pleasantly surprised to find themselves seated with President and Mrs. Bush who easily conversed throughout the meal with humor and grace. The event was a perfect blend of all that the Bushes loved most about their two home states, Texas and Maine.

Afterwards, it was time to preview the Maine exhibit. President Bush accompanied our group, flattered we would travel so far and beaming with delight to share the special event with his Kennebunkport friends. I, too, was filled with pride to have been a small part of our hometown exhibition on display for the world to see. (I later went on to intern at the George Bush Presidential Library and Museum, a surreal experience I continue to cherish.) The rest of the trip was filled with many more special moments and memories. President and Mrs. Bush were the most gracious hosts, always exuding warmth, friendship and humor. They were honorable, genuine, larger-than-life souls who brought out the best in those who surround them. President Bush epitomized how to live a kind and meaningful life, one that truly blessed our community, and will forever remain an important chapter in our local history.

Rebecca Bradbury Roberts

On a beautiful morning in September 2006, Tom Bradbury and I were comfortably seated in the warm and inviting living room of President Bush's Walker's Point estate. The windows before us offered a spectacular view of the Atlantic. On a large, nearby coffee table I had set up a tape recorder and tested it to make sure that it was working. We were there as part of a Kennebunkport Historical Society oral history project for which the president had consented to be interviewed.

President Bush was all smiles when he came into the room to greet us. He settled down in his favorite chair. I explained our procedure and then turned on the recorder.

For the next hour we moved from one question to another. We asked about his earliest childhood memories, his friends, where he played and similar questions. The time passed quickly but before we ended one final question was asked.

"Mr. President," I queried, "in many ways you've answered this already, but it strikes me that you've been everywhere. You've met so many people and been to so many beautiful places. What keeps you coming back to Kennebunkport?"

"It's all about family and the familiar," he replied. "I look over in that corner," he said pointing to the opposite wall, "and I see my grandfather, at nighttime, a tie still on, playing solitaire. And I look out on those rocks," he turned to point towards the sea, "and one of them is our submarine, and we're kids and we're playing." This was home.

As we were getting up to go, the president said that he wanted to show us *Wandby Cottage*, a guesthouse that had been recently renovated. As we stepped out on the porch he paused and pointed to a sign that read "CAVU." "That's what my life is now, ceiling and visibility unlimited. It goes back to when I was a pilot," he explained. "We didn't have the instruments they have today. We relied a lot on sight, and when the air was clear and the visibility unlimited it was a great day and the best flying of all." His meaning was clear. Life was good.

We all climbed into a golf cart and he drove us over to the cottage, which he proudly showed us before driving us back to our car. It had been an exciting morning, meaningful and enjoyable, and we hoped as we drove away that the recording we made would properly reflect this remarkable chapter in our town's history.

Robert Card

I first came to know George H.W. Bush when he came into our one-hour camera shop and photo studio, *Ocean Exposure*, which was located in Lower Village, Kennebunk, a short drive from his home at Walker's Point. Mrs. Bush was an avid photographer and frequent customer and on occasion he would come into the shop with her. They were always delightfully friendly and very down to earth. You can imagine the buzz that occurred from time to time during his presidency when other customers were in the shop and the full entourage of the president and his Secret Service detail would show up to pick up film or some prints.

As we got to know them well, we had the opportunity to photograph President and Mrs. Bush on many occasions throughout the next 25 plus years, starting during his presidency. Over the years I was inspired by this caring, giving, humble man. I don't ever recall him saying no to

anyone who asked for an autograph or a photo. He was very patient and always accommodating. He also liked adventure. He was especially fond of motoring— perhaps the better word is rocketing— around the waters off Kennebunkport in his cigarette boat *Fidelity*.

One day I received a call saying that the president would like some photos with his boat. I was instructed to meet him down at the Yachtsman Hotel on the river in Kennebunkport where he moored his boat. I appeared at the dock at the designated time loaded with cameras and ready to go. He had other friends aboard, including Nancy Sosa, who shared many such outings with the president. Once we hit the open Atlantic, *Fidelity* was put on maximum speed, which is about 70 miles per hour—I'm not sure what that translates to in knots but let's say it was VERY fast! As we're flying over the waves, I'm photographing away, struggling to

Over the years I was inspired by this caring, giving, humble man.

keep my balance while the guests held on for dear life. The president loved speed. After motoring around the open water for some time, we soon headed toward the cove at Walker's Point, again at full speed. I'm shooting away when the president unexpectedly decides to pull one of his signature turns, which involved cutting the helm while the boat is roaring along at hair raising speed. One of my cameras, which didn't have as good a grip as I did, hit me with a crack in my side. I ended up with a broken rib. I said nothing, of course. After we docked, the President and Mrs, Bush—she had not been aboard as she had long before decided that trips in *Fidelity* were a bit too raucous for her taste—gave Nancy Sosa and me an impromptu tour of the Big House at Walker's Point. They took the time to show us the photos on the walls depicting historical moments while telling stories about each image. The tour even included his new state-of-the-

art Kohler computerized shower as well as the third floor commode, which the president claimed had the best view in Kennebunkport. I was impressed with their graciousness and kindness. It felt like we were hanging out with the neighbors. They both had a great sense of humor and he told some entertaining stories from his youth at Walker's Point.

At the end of the tour they gave us each a stack of plastic cups with the presidential seal. Then, just like any long married couple, Mrs. Bush turned to the president and said "George what are we having for dinner?" "I don't know, Bar," he replied. "How about we cook something up on the grill?"

I had such a good time that I hardly noticed my broken rib until I got home.

Chris Smith

61

FUN

It was the summer of 1995. My 10-year-old friend Jason Gagnon and I were scrambling along the Kennebunk River jetty hoping to lure crabs with a mussel clothes-pinned to the end of a string. We looked up to see the president's famous cigarette boat, *Fidelity*, making a slow curve right by us.

Jason called out, "Hello, Mr. President!"

A grinning George H. W. Bush shouted back, "Hey, dude!"

My young friend went white. "Bethe, the president called me dude. He called me dude!!!"

Bethe Hagens

Years ago, then Vice President Bush asked me to go fishing off the coast of Maine. It is always a perilous journey to navigate through the lobster pots but even more so at full throttle in the vice president's powerful boat *Fidelity*. We were only a short way from Walker's Point when we heard a grinding sound.

The vice president brought his boat to a hard stop and said, "I think the engine's entangled with a lobster pot line."

Before anyone could react, he stripped off his shirt and shoes and dove in the icy water in his long pants to unwind the rope from the engine. The Secret Service was caught off guard when he said, "I'll take care of it."

Ten minutes later we were underway.

Debbie Stapleton

During a mid-July tour in 2010, as I was driving the tourist Intown Trolley around Narragansett Point for the return trip past Gooch's Beach, I saw a sight I'd never seen before: a boat stranded at the north end of the beach—actually on the beach. After pointing out the sighting to the tourists on board, I uttered, "Ya know, that almost looks like President Bush's boat." Then I caught myself, "Omigosh, it is! And there's the president on the beach with a crowd around him!" Everyone snapped photos as quickly as they could.

As soon as my tours for the day ended and I gassed up the trolley and returned it to its overnight home at the barn, I sought out my neighbor who operated 41's chase-boat.

"What happened?" I inquired.

"Well," he explained, "the president and Barbara went to *Barnacle Billy's* in Ogunquit for lunch in his boat. Because the boat ride over was a bit rough, Barbara chose to come back by motorcade, while 41 took his boat. On the way back a huge fog came in from nowhere. Zero visibility. He cut his engine and was preparing to assist another boater nearby, when a wave brought his boat onto the beach; and because the tide was receding, we couldn't get it off."

Later that night on the NBC News, in a teaser just before the last break, the host said, "And when we come back, we'll show you how a president beached his boat today."

I heard that after the news report, needless to say, he received numerous, humorous, telephone calls from his many friends, ribbing the life out of him.

Jack Savona

My family's restaurant, *Barnacle Billy's* in Perkins Cove, Ogunquit, was a favorite spot for President George H.W. Bush and his wife Barbara. I called him George because he asked us to.

We would get a phone call from the Secret Service about two hours before his arrival alerting us that George was on his way in *Fidelity* to have lunch at his favorite table on the deck. Our staff and customers waited in excited anticipation for the Bushes to arrive.

We've been serving the Bushes and a variety of their famous guests for years, including President Bill Clinton and New England Patriots legend Tom Brady.

Our father and the president had a lot of the same values and a real connection. The Bushes felt very comfortable here at *Barnacle Billy's*. George's favorite was our steamers. Billy showed him his special way of enjoying clams by tipping them in broth, then red wine vinegar, again in steaming hot broth and then lastly dipping them in hot butter. The president loved it and never ate them any other way.

The president also loved feeding the stripers swimming under our deck so we would give him a supply of raw hamburger to keep the fish happy.

When my father died, George wrote a letter to my family. It was a a true act of kindness which accurately described the man we knew and miss here at *Billy's*.

My family and our community were honored to know and to serve the Bushes at our restaurant. Even though he was once the Leader of the Free World, we will always remember him as down-to-earth George.

Cathy (Tower) Koppstein
Co-owner, Barnacle Billy's

It was a privilege to always greet George, Barbara and their family. It always made our day here at *Barnacle Billy's*. He was a pure gentleman with a wonderful sense of kindness and a great sense of humor.

Meg Tower
Co-owner, Barnacle Billy's

For all of us who live in the Kennebunks and love the water, the Kennebunk River has played a significant role in our lives. Two people, in particular, who have made a huge impact in town and on the river come to mind.

As young boys they loved to race each other down the river in their boats, one a local, the other a summer resident. Booth Chick, the local, became known for his craftsmanship, building lobster boats and the coveted Chickee sailboats. He was founder of *Chick's Marina*. He could build or fix just about anything for anybody.

The other individual became a congressman, ambassador, CIA director, vice president, and 41st President of the United States. With all their achievements, they were at heart locals who simply loved the Kennebunk River.

When Booth passed away, a group of citizens decided that he should be recognized with a bench installed at Government Wharf where Booth's truck was sighted every evening watching activities on the river. President Bush was first on board with the project. For the dedication of the bench he arrived dressed in Booth Chick red pants and navy shirt, his final tribute to a childhood friend. The bench remains there today for all to enjoy.

President Bush's love of the river continued through his presidential years. Oftentimes, a round of golf at Cape Arundel Golf Club preceded a few casts into the river. If a rainy day wiped out the golf it was still perfect for casting the river for striped bass.

One adventure started with a 5am meeting to fish the Kennebunk in my 12-foot boat made by my old friend Booth.

Together, the president and I fished the river from the basin to the golf course. What made it interesting was the Secret Service and Coast Guard flotilla that followed us as well as watching the press from around the world doing their jobs making sure they didn't miss a thing. It was quite a sight watching the reporters walking the river shore in their Gucci shoes and sport coats getting covered in seaweed and slapping at mosquitoes.

The president loved his time on the water, whether as a young boy racing his friends or as a former president cruising the river or the ocean in *Fidelity*.

Ken Raynor
PGA Professional

Once upon a time, there was job in the White House called the Horseshoe Commissioner. You might be surprised to know such a position existed...but it did, at least unofficially, according to President George H.W. Bush.

Early in his presidency, I was the White House Horseshoe Commissioner. Twenty-one years old, fresh out of college, and a new member of the president's small personal staff, I was in way over my head. And the president, he was passionate about playing horseshoes. It was something he played with his family and friends, visiting heads of state, celebrities and members of Congress. It was also his way to unwind, break the ice, do casual business, or just to get the competitive juices flowing.

The "pit" was conveniently located behind the Oval Office next to the White House swimming pool. It was his creation—something not seen at the White House since Harry Truman. And there was a whole foreign language associated with his horseshoe play. Phrases like "Vic Damone!" for a win, "Ugly Shoe!" for a bad toss, or "Power Outage!" for a horseshoe that failed to reach the clay. He was "Mr. Smooth" when he'd throw a ringer.

On occasion, I would be called by President Bush from my normal duties to officiate a match or render a ruling on whether a throw was, in fact, a ringer or which shoe was closer to the stake. Calipers were used to measure which horseshoe got the coveted point. In time, I earned a moniker from him, "The Commissioner," finding the president jokingly credentialing my "integrity" to his opponent of the day. He would announce

regally that I was "fair and just" and that my rulings had never been reversed by the "Horseshoe Czar"—him.

The president hosted two horseshoe tournaments for the staff each year: The Fall Classic and the Sweet Sixteen Invitational. With multiple rounds and a loser's bracket, each tournament would last about a month. They were legendary. The job of the White House Horseshoe Commissioner was to help him pull off those events. Staff teams of two competed for all the glory. But it was not the staff you might expect. At the insistence of the president, teams came from the unsung offices that make the White House tick: the White House electricians, butlers, groundskeepers, motorpool, chefs, ushers, carpenters, marine sentries, and Secret Service details all had teams. So, too, did the president and his son, Marvin. Mrs. Bush would set the brackets, in a semi-formal ceremony, by pulling teams randomly out of a ballcap.

The president was competitive too. He would want briefings on specific matches in the tournament and scouting reports on opponents. In 1990, only moments before he was to welcome Soviet leader Mikhail Gorbachev at an official state visit ceremony on the South Lawn, our small staff was standing with the president just outside the Oval Office. As he got ready to walk across the Rose Garden to meet Mr. Gorbachev, President Bush turned back to ask who he was playing in the second round of the tournament and wanted me to get a scouting report on the electricians. After the president unexpectedly lost to those same electricians in a sweep, I ran into his steward Domingo in the hall of the

The President trying out the royal gift as Her Majesty Queen Elizabeth looks on.

It was his daily example of grace that made us want to be better people.

West Wing. "The president very, very upset" he told me. "Bad mood. He lose at horseshoes."

The best horseshoe team was the Housemen, led by Ron Jones, a man with the swagger and physique of an NFL lineman. One evening before the big semifinals the trash talking reached a crescendo and the president (who was already out of the tournament), had enough. He shed his suit coat to take on Ron mano-a-mano in a one-game grudge match to see who was the "King of the Pit." It lasted just 5 minutes and the president won 21-0. The next day, the president teased him, "Ron I just want to know, did I make you nervous, you know, playing the President of the United States?" It might have been his greatest horseshoe victory. A photo from that day hung in the kitchen of his post-presidency office in Houston.

For the finals of the tournaments, he would invite the staff and their families to the White House to watch in person. Awards would be presented. I remember a "No Broccoli" shirt. More good-natured teasing might ensue. Perhaps an impromptu match with the president himself might break out. The winner had their name engraved on a wooden horseshoe box that would end up at the Presidential Library. It all had the feel of a family barbeque.

At one of the finals, as the sun went down, the president worried that the women attending were getting cold and went to find sweatshirts to warm them. At the conclusion of another, a longtime member of the ushers' office came to me excitedly. In all his years in the White House, he had never been invited to anything but a Christmas reception. He said that afternoon was the most thrilling moment of his 45 years of service. Those were the little moments that mattered to George Bush.

Former senior advisor and friend Ron Kaufman said it best, President Bush was "master of the small gesture." The handwritten note, a word of thanks, his endearing humor, the show of concern for a person hurting. Everyone who knew or worked for him was touched by him in a way that likely improved the trajectory of their life. It was his daily example of grace that made us want to be better people. It still does.

On my last day in the White House, he asked me into the Oval Office and presented those same horseshoe calipers mounted on a block of wood, with the inscription, "White House Horseshoe Commissioner 1989-1990: His rulings have never been reversed." The master of the small gesture.

The president's greatness, leadership and generosity will be written about for years by the amazing men and women who helped him make history. The fall of the Berlin Wall, the unification of Germany, the liberation of Kuwait, the Americans with Disabilities Act. As a young aide with a front-row seat, I was a blessed observer

doing my bit to help a good man but I was not one who truly helped make history. However, when it comes to horseshoes, well, that's a different story. That's a story I can write.

Horseshoes at the White House was the perfect embodiment of George H.W. Bush. Competitive, yet considerate. A sense of humor and light-heartedness brought to a deadly serious job. And more importantly, a way to make the oftentimes-overlooked people feel special. Every person was important to him. The definition of decency.

One of the last times I saw the president was in Houston a few years ago, when I brought my two children to his office to meet him for the first time. Parkinson's made it hard for him to speak. My son and daughter were standing on either side of his wheelchair, just the two of them and the president. My wife and I were a few feet away talking to his aide, when the president pulled the kids down close and said in a hushed whisper, "I love your dad." The ultimate small gesture. Today, those same kids, now young adults, pitch shoes at our cabin high in mountains of Montana. On some nights as the sun sets and the stars begin to emerge, I might watch them from the back deck and think about him.

At his funeral, sitting in the National Cathedral, I fought back tears as the majestic church bells tolled outside. Only the sound I heard was subtly different. It sounded more like the sweet clanking of horseshoes on a warm, spring evening. It was the sound of the greatest man I ever knew.

Brian Yablonski
Executive Director
Property and Environment Research Center (PERC)
Bozeman, Montana

The President always thought of the other guy and that day was no different. His love of people, the sea, and the game of golf all rolled into a cherished memory for all of us.

With President Bush, it was always about faith, family, and friends first in his life. Not far behind was his compassion for the other guy, time on the water, fishing and sports. He loved tennis and golf and played both with enthusiasm during his time in Kennebunkport.

As the Head PGA Golf Professional at Cape Arundel Golf Club we spent many an hour together playing and practicing golf. We also shared a love of the sea and fishing, so many a tale was shared during this cherished friendship.

I remember one adventure, in particular, that combined several of his interests into one story. The Maine Amateur Golf Championship was being played nearby at the Biddeford Saco Country Club.

Playing in this championship was a dear friend and multiple-time champion Mark Plummer as well as Cape Arundel Golf Club's own and defending champion Eric Higgins.

In true form a phone call came from President Bush.

"Kenny, we must go and cheer our boys on. Can you make it?"

Can anyone say no to that? I told him I would be happy to go.

"Meet at the boat at 10," he said, and the phone line cut off.

Off we went joined by Stephen Spenlinhauer, another good friend who has shared many adventures with the president. It was full speed in *Fidelity* to the Saco River, just a few miles north of Kennebunkport by water. We motored up the river to the dock where we were met by 41's motorcade, which took us to the course.

The crowd was abuzz! After all, the president was on hand cheering on Mark and Eric. I'm sure the sight of the cart driven by the 41st President of the United States influenced their concentration.

After the rounds were completed we all shared a quick lunch and many golf stories. Eric had not defended his title successfully so he was feeling disappointed. Our president knew the remedy.

"Eric, we came by boat and I think a good fast ride home for you will help you forget the round," said 41. So Eric hopped aboard for the ride of his life. It was full speed with hair flying. Sure enough, a big smile creased Eric's face and he seemed to forget all about those bad drives and missed putts.

The president always thought of the other guy and that day was no different. His love of people, the sea, and the game of golf all rolled into a cherished memory for all of us.

Ken Raynor
PGA Professional
Cape Arundel Golf Club

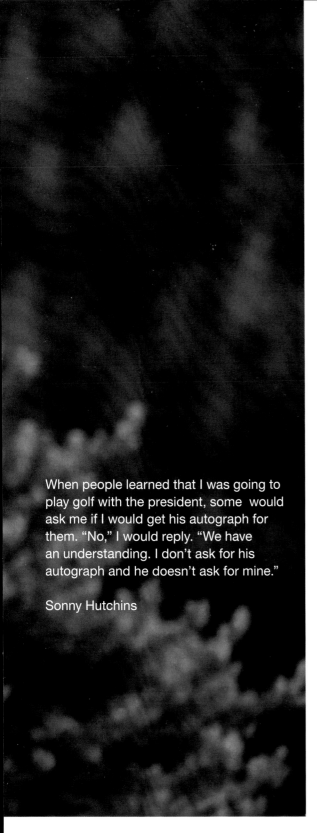

When people learned that I was going to play golf with the president, some would ask me if I would get his autograph for them. "No," I would reply. "We have an understanding. I don't ask for his autograph and he doesn't ask for mine."

Sonny Hutchins

I was fortunate to be part of a group of women who for many years enjoyed an annual reunion in Kennebunkport called "the summit." During one summit about 15 years ago, when we met President Bush on the golf course, he invited us to Walker's Point for a dog-eat-dog putting contest. That day, he dubbed us the "summiteers", a name which has lived on.

Over the years President Bush invited the summiteers to "Camp Walker's Point" for boat trips, Segway rides, laps in the pool, etc. My personal favorite was the time he arranged for us to meet legendary golfer Phil Mickelson, or as I call him, "my Phil." Once President Bush realized that one of the summiteers was a huge Phil Mickelson fan, there was no stopping him.

It was during a game of horseshoes at Walker's Point between the president and Phil when the meeting occurred. It was unforgettable, as was President Bush's thoughtfulness in making it happen.

How much did the summiteers love President Bush? Enough to toil in the kitchen for hours, creating a huge chocolate mess in a desire to make the best Eskimo Pies ever for the Eskimo Pie-loving former president. If you have never made Eskimo Pies, don't! It was all worth it, though, when we learned that President Bush gave our efforts a big thumbs up.

Sally Sweeney
Summiteer

It was the year that President and Mrs. Bush came back to Kennebunkport to celebrate Christmas Prelude for the first time. This annual holiday celebration, which started 38 years ago, is known nationwide but, as summer residents, the Bushes had never taken part.

Friends of ours, Kavin and Virginia Moody and Lee and Mary White, sat with my husband Bob and I eating an Italian dinner of baked penne with lots of meatballs and sauce. Lee looked out and saw an SUV coming up the driveway of our art gallery, which shared space in our house. Then President Bush and Barbara came walking down the hallway. They had just come from the Christmas caroling event at the nearby Franciscan Monastery. President Bush said, "Boy does that smell good, I wish we hadn't made reservations for dinner." Then he added, "We came by to wish all of you a very Merry Christmas!" And then Lee said, "Mr. President, you and Mrs. Bush coming by to wish us a Merry Christmas has made my Christmas."

The president thought for a moment and then said, "If our coming by here to wish you a Merry Christmas made your Christmas, you had better get a life."

Of course, we all had a great laugh and lots of hugs. And it did make our Christmas.

Evelyn and Bob Paine

One very special day President Bush, Barbara and their son, Jeb, stopped by our art gallery accompanied by the famous golfer Arnold Palmer and his wife. They wanted to see the newest four by eight oil painting that Bob had finished for friends of ours who had been collecting his paintings for several years. Our friends had a condo a couple of blocks away so we invited everyone to walk over to see the painting. My daughter and her husband came along as well. The condo is on Maine Street close to some guest houses. The guests were looking out of the windows, amazed to see the Bushes and the Palmers walking by. They called out with many words of congratulations. I am sure, like us, it made their day.

Evelyn Paine

80 FENWAY P

Years ago when President Bush was vice president, he was in Concord, New Hampshire campaigning for the Presidency. At the time, my husband Bob and I were living in both New Hampshire and in Kennebunkport.

The vice president called us and invited us to visit him at the office where he planned to greet the people of Concord and the surrounding towns. Of course, we couldn't wait to see him so we drove right down to the office. When we arrived we were startled and thrilled to find Red Sox legend Ted Williams visiting with him. I couldn't believe it! As a teenager I was a big fan of the Red Sox and Ted Williams was my hero. I was in shock!

To be introduced to Ted Williams by the vice president—it just couldn't get any better!

The first thing I blurted out to Ted was, "I was at Fenway Park the day you hit three home runs. I was the teenager sitting behind home plate yelling, 'You can do it, Ted!' And you did it!"

I have never forgotten either day, the one at Fenway Park and meeting Ted Williams in Concord. I thanked President Bush many times over the years for that treat. Bob never forgot that day either. President Bush introduced him to Ted as, "Meet Bob Paine, a favorite artist of our family!"

Evelyn Paine

President Bush had an appreciative spirit, which was demonstrated by his innumerable thank you letters sent to so many people. I treasure his cards of gratitude for my gift to him of colorful socks as well as my participation in his son Jeb's campaign for the presidency. The indomitable Jean Becker, the president's longtime chief of staff, set up campaign headquarters at the Kennebunkport Inn where I joined his Houston clan and many others who showed up from all over the country to campaign in New Hampshire.

Had I not been called to babysitting duties for our granddaughters, I would have been one of the lucky ones to stand on the grounds of St. Ann's Episcopal Church when he parachuted down with a roar celebrating his 90th year.

His many Kennebunkport friends will miss their special movie nights in Saco with the President and Mrs. Bush. Their vibrant personalities and loving spirit will always remain with us in the Port community.

Katie Pressly

On a spectacular Maine day in August of 2006 the first Bush/Sosa picnic was held on Stage Island in Cape Porpoise, which is just a short boat ride east of Walker's Point. President Bush mischievously referred to the event as the "B/S picnic."

I was in Kennebunkport with my 16-year-old stepdaughter, Jamie, visiting the Sosas. A bunch of friends and family gathered in boats and met out at Stage Island for the picnic. President Bush, in his usual fashion, organized sporting events. One was a kayak race. Jamie was hesitant about doing her lap, so Nick Sosa volunteered to do it for her. However, at the last minute she changed her mind. She paddled at top speed out to the marker and back again, arriving at the beach to President Bush cheering, "Way to go Jamie! You really hauled ass!"

He loved to make little irreverent and un-presidential remarks.

Susan Biddle

Lucy Sosa, 10, and Jamie Barkin, 11, with President Bush. We had been invited to the Point for cocktails when Mrs. Bush took this photo. When I showed this photo to my mom, then in her eighties, she said about President Bush, "Some shirt!"

Women of Note, a Kennebunk-based a capella singing group founded in 1991, was blessed to sing for 41 for the past couple decades at many special gatherings at Walker's Point. This allowed us to rub shoulders and sing with many famous performers, including the *Oak Ridge Boys* with whom we performed an a capella arrangement of *Amazing Grace* that gave me goosebumps. We even performed at a Presidential Library dinner at the Kennebunk River Club and sang at The White House during 43's Presidential tenure. One of the highlights for us was when we sang to 41 and Mrs. Bush just prior to 41 getting on the airplane to jump on his 90th birthday (photo at left). We were filmed by the Today show as we performed that morning so I experienced some "fearbumps" of my own.

We also sang for the president on his 94th birthday for a small gathering of his family shortly after his beloved Barbara's passing. Our goal was to choose songs that would put a smile on his face, rather than tears. Our song list included *Boogie Woogie Bugle Boy*, *Devoted to You* and *Lean on Me*. Unfortunately, tears came to everyone's eyes shortly after the first notes of *Devoted to You* were sung.

For me, the genuine kindness of 41 and his First Lady was shown in a very personal way when they invited me over to Walker's Point for a hug after my husband passed away. That is one afternoon, along with a lifetime of memories, I will never forget.

Lisa Mills

For ten summers I drove the Intown Trolley around Kennebunkport and Kennebunk Beach, narrating the tour along the way. Some days, when we passed the Bush compound at Walker's Point, if the crowd seemed attentive and receptive, I would say, "I must've driven out there at least 20 or 25 times for cocktails." When the trolley riders seemed duly impressed, I would add, "Oh, did I mention each time I was driving the trolley, and the people on the trolley got to actually have the cocktails while I waited for them?" Invariably, someone would yell out, "I knew it was something like that."

Prior to one of those afternoon charter trips to Walker's Point, one of my Secret Service neighbors told me that 41 had just received delivery of a new *Fidelity V* fishing/speedboat that was three feet longer and quite a bit faster than the one before, which was already outfitted with three 300 horsepower engines.

Shortly thereafter I was on a charter out to Walker's Point and, as the president's guests boarded the trolley for the ride back to their dinner venue, 41 walked one of his guests back to the trolley. As he approached me he extended me his right hand, which he had done once before, and casually said, "Hi, I'm George Bush."

"Hi! I'm Jack Savona," I replied, never indicating that we had met before under the same circumstances.

As he stood next to me, I uttered, "I understand you've got a new toy."

"A new toy?" he responded, seeming a bit puzzled. "Oh, you mean *Fidelity*! Oh, yes! Why it's three feet longer than *Fidelity IV* and much faster."

As he related his excitement about his new boat, he put his left arm around my shoulder and I instinctively put my right arm around his waist. We were just two locals sharing a story.

While the president related the details of the boat, I heard Chris Smith, a local photographer, clicking away with his digital camera behind me. The next day I asked Chris if he would email one of the photos of me with the president, which he did. It's a photograph I treasure, even though you can't see either of our faces. You can, however, recognize 41 by his tall, statesmanlike stance and me by my bald spot next to him. It's a photograph I treasure and will pass on to my grandchildren, along with this story.

Jack Savona

Almost 30 years ago I was playing golf with Kennebunkport resident and long-time pal Sandy Boardman at Cape Arundel Golf Club. "Playing golf" is stretching it, because I was a complete novice with two lessons under my visor.

We were on the back nine. I hit a drive that somehow actually got airborne but landed in a thicket bordering the fairway. As Sandy drove the cart towards where we thought my ball might be, she said, "Don't worry, the president is playing here today so I know the Secret Service have probably already spotted your ball."

They had, and so had President Bush and his playing partner, CBS sportscaster Jim Nantz.

Sandy, a longtime friend and fishing partner of 41, greeted the men and introduced me. Apparently, the president's ball had landed in the same thicket.

"You go ahead and hit your ball first," he said graciously.

"Oh no, please, you go," I said.

"Absolutely not," he answered.

I desperately didn't want to whiff, skull or shank the ball as I'd been doing for the past dozen holes. Amazingly, miraculously, I managed to hit the pink *Flying Lady* up and over a group of boulders, through two trees, around a shrub and right back into the center of the fairway.

"Great shot!" he said. Little did he know, but then again, I think he did.

And as we drove off, I wondered—and still do to this day—exactly where his errant shot ended up next.

Valerie Marier

87

One day my husband Bob answered the phone and passed it to me. "It's the president," he said, as if I received calls from the White House all the time. "He wants to talk with you."

Thinking he was kidding, I took the phone and said, "Hello?"

"Hello Mrs. Preble," came a familiar voice. "This is George Bush. Barbara and I have talked it over and feel we would like to be buried in Arundel Cemetery. I was given your name to call."

"Yes," I replied, shaking just a bit. "I am Clerk of the cemetery." We then set a date and time when he could see a possible lot. As I hung up the phone I couldn't wait to attend the next meeting of the Arundel Cemetery Board to share the news.

We had just completed a new area on the hill near the North Congregational Church and it was all groomed and ready to sell. But, I asked myself, is it attractive enough for the president and first lady?

Our Sexton, Wilbur "Wib" Cluff and his brother John got right on it, and by the time President Bush was due to arrive all the improvements that could be made had been made.

Wib and I had grown up together at the Town House, and though my surname was Clough, we were cousins. We had attended the Town House School and had often ridden our bikes on the winding dirt roads of the cemetery. On the day that we were scheduled to meet the president, Wib and I were waiting in his pickup truck on one of those dirt roads, keeping a close watch on the cemetery entrance. We didn't have long to wait, for soon several shiny black cars with their lights on turned through the gate. In one of those cars we knew sat the President of the United States. Wib looked at me and said, "Lou, if only our fathers could see us now!"

We led the entourage to the special area we wanted the president to see, and as soon as we came to a stop the

president darted out of the back seat of one of those cars and came our way. He shook hands with Wib and me and then immediately headed off in the opposite direction, reading out the engraved names on the monument stones as he went. "Longley Philbrick," he exclaimed, "He rebuilt our house after the hurricane. Good man. Excellent carpenter!" Dashing across the road he yelled out, "Booth Chick. He taught me how to sail! I miss Booth. We were good friends."

Wib and I looked at each other wondering if the president was going to cover the entire cemetery. Many of his friends were buried there and that could take some time. However, the president soon realized that we were waiting for him and returned to look over the lot we had suggested.

"I'm sure Barbara will think this place is just fine," he said. "Thank you. I'll be in touch." And then Wib and I watched wide-eyed as everyone drove off.

It wasn't all that long before I received another call from the president. We were on a first name basis then as he said, "Luverne, Barbara and I will not be using the attractive burial lot in Arundel Cemetery that we chose a while back.

"It seems that the powers to be have decided that we should be buried at the library that's being built in College Station, Texas. There will be a cement walkway leading up to the gravesite there. It's probably for the best because people would have been tramping all over your beautiful place and making a mess of things. But thank you!"

He was probably right. Our little cemetery could have never have handled the traffic brought by a presidential burial. But it will always please me to know that at least his heart is here, among friends.

Luverne Preble

89

It was a memorable first visit from the president— one that would be repeated often over the years as we socialized over the exchange of blueberry pies.

It was May of 1994 and we had recently moved into our new house on Ocean Avenue not far from Walker's Point. It was a cold and wet morning—spring in Maine—and I had returned from a grocery shopping expedition to the local market. Brown bags were scattered all over the kitchen floor and counter tops. I was barefoot and my hair was wet. Chilled, I took a quick look out of the kitchen window hoping for a glimpse of the weatherman's promised break in the weather.

There was a Secret Service agent standing at the end of the driveway.

At that precise moment President George H.W. Bush rang our front doorbell. I answered. He introduced himself as our neighbor, handed me a gift bottle of California champagne—how perfect—and I invited him in for a tour of our newly constructed home. He nodded to the Secret Service agent and in he came. We spent a lovely half hour as I gave him a tour of the house, which really smelled of wet brown paper bags. I, of course, was still barefoot. My long departed mother would have been horrified. The president mentioned that he had recently met good friends of ours at a Colby College event and we chatted about this mutual connection.

He made all the appropriate kind comments about the new house—the bathroom soaking tubs, the backyard rusted tin sculptures—and gave apologies for Barbara who was off on another errand, and with another handshake he was off. I was left limp and charmed.

It was a memorable first visit from the president—one that would be repeated often over the years as we socialized over the exchange of blueberry pies, packages of specialized photo paper, traded books and movie tapes. I think his tape library still has our copy of *Young Frankenstein*. His welcome note that accompanied the bottle of champagne, framed, still graces the entrance to our home.

What a grand man. What grand years and memories. No words do those two wonderful people justice. They were fabulous neighbors, Americans, and world citizens. We were honored to see them out and about in our town.

Maxine and Herb Weintraub

Although I had been photographing him for several years at locations throughout the Kennebunks, including at the Memorial Day Parade or at St. Ann's Church, I actually met George H.W. Bush for the first time in 1999 when I was part of a group of locals who traveled to his presidential library in College Station, Texas, for the opening of a special exhibit dedicated to Kennebunkport. Several of my photos were part of the exhibit.

When I published the first edition of a book *Kennebunkport: A Photographic Tour* in 2004, he invited me to Walker's Point. From then on, he would recognize and greet me whenever we would see each other. I remember once at the conclusion of an event at the Nonantum Resort, a Kennebunkport institution, he warmed my heart by introducing me to the person he was with by saying "This guy takes really great photos of Kennebunkport."

Every year, I would send him a copy of my latest *Images of Kennebunkport* calendar and soon would follow one of his precious handwritten notes. In these notes, he commented on a wide range of subjects, sometimes referring to my family and nearly always talking about how much he passionately loved Walker's Point and Kennebunkport. He seemed to have a unique ability to say in a few well-chosen words what others might take several sentences to say. When he wrote to me that "You truly know how to capture all the beauty in this small town", I knew that no one had ever said anything nicer about my photography and that no one ever would. I was just one of hundreds of people locally and thousands of people worldwide who received personal notes from President Bush, but I cherish every one of them and will pass them down to my children as the historical documents they are.

Robert Dennis

I had the honor of working in the Advance Office of the White House during the fours years of President George H.W. Bush's Administration. During that time I had the opportunity to visit Kennebunkport for a Pre-Advance trip. A lot of time has passed since then and I was able to return in 2018 for a final farewell. I knew the president was in failing health but I was still hopeful that my husband and my daughters could join me in seeing him for a brief visit at Walker's Point. It was a bittersweet day. While enjoying the stunning view of the ocean from his home, we learned that the president was not feeling well that day and could not accept any visitors. Still, we enjoyed walking the grounds and taking in the salt air but there was a definite sense that things were just not the same without Barbara Bush there.

Lucy Muckerman Lamb

My wife Shirley was cleaning up the kitchen when the phone rang. "Hi, is this Shirley?" the caller asked in a friendly and familiar voice. When she replied in the affirmative he continued, "This is George Bush. I was wondering if you and Tom would consider joining us for dinner next Friday night."

For Shirley, this raised room for doubt on several levels. During the course of the average week we would receive dozens of calls, the kids mostly, checking in or catching up. My mother had us on speed dial. Telemarketers seemed to have our number despite our best attempts to block them out. Work related questions, the occasional crisis, bill collectors, wrong numbers, none of them would have seemed unlikely or out of the question; none that is except a call from a former President of the United States. Then there was the question of dinner. My cousin and I owned a tiny grocery store in Kennebunkport, and I was the head of the small local land trust, a group dedicated towards preserving the local landscape. The President and Mrs. Bush were faithful customers of the store and very generous supporters of the Trust. They were wonderfully inclusive with the townspeople they knew and would include us sometimes in an event that was happening or a gathering they thought we might enjoy. On those occasions we might receive an invitation in the mail or a call from a staff intern. This was different. It was either my cousin Russell playing a cruel joke, she thought, or the unlikely but real thing. She went with the latter.

"We would love to Mr. President," she replied sincerely, and continuing as she would if any other friend had placed the invitation. She asked, "Would you like us to bring anything?"

"No, no," the president chuckled, "I think we're all set in that regard. Why don't you come over at six o'clock?"

"We'll look forward to it," Shirley responded as they said their goodbyes. And we did look forward to it. The rest of the week passed quickly.

It is about a 15-minute ride from our house to the Bushes beloved family compound on Walker's Point, built around 1900 by the president's grandfather. We had been to a few cocktail parties there in the past so we were somewhat familiar with how the flow of events went. The Secret Service maintained a checkpoint at the entrance to the property. We would stop there, our names would be checked off a list and then we would follow the flow of other guests to determine where to park and go. But as we approached the gate, something was disturbingly unfamiliar. There were no other guests to follow. A disquieting question crossed my mind.

"Shirley," I asked as I slowed the car and steered to the side of the driveway. "Are you sure he said Friday night?"

"I think he said Friday night," she replied.

"You think? You think?" I said almost to myself. "Actually, this is one of those times when 'I'm sure' would be a much more comforting answer."

"Well," she said, "how about this? I'm sure that I think it was Friday night." It wasn't quite what I was looking for, but it was all I had so I continued on to the checkpoint.

94

"Good evening," the agent said as he stepped out of the booth to meet us.

"Good evening," I replied as I rolled down the car window. I gave him our names and said that we had been invited over for dinner.

"One moment please," he said as he returned to his station and looked over a clipboard. The process took a bit longer than I had hoped. I saw him picking up a phone and asking questions of someone. A few minutes later he returned with some unsettling news. "I'm sorry Mr. Bradbury, but you're not on our list for tonight. Let me call up to the house." As he left a new thought occurred to me. "Are you sure that it was this Friday?" I asked Shirley.

"I'm pretty sure he said next Friday which I presume is this Friday," she responded, "but it all happened so unexpectedly." This was awkward.

It seemed like an hour, but it was actually just a couple of minutes before the agent came back to say, "They say to have you go on to the house."

"Did they say anything about a dinner?" I wanted to know.

"No, sir," was the reply. "They just said for you to go up to the house." He then told me where to park and wished us a pleasant evening.

We continued slowly past the gate that had been opened then on to the house. All was quiet there, too quiet. Another Secret Service agent was nearby and I asked him where I should go. He pointed us to the front door and said that we should just knock. From the doorstep we could see through to the living room.

President Bush was there, seated in a beautifully upholstered chair. Across from him was Barbara. Both were reading, looking as though they were comfortably settled in for the evening. I was shaken with another wave of doubt. "This just can't be right," I told Shirley. "Let's see if we can find Ariel."

Ariel DeGuzman was the Bush's trusted family steward who had been with them since their years at the White House. He would know what's going on, I thought. If we had come on the wrong night he would help us get out of the mistake without a complete loss of pride. I had delivered groceries to the kitchen in the past and beat a path to that door, hoping that he would be there. Thankfully, he was.

"Ariel," I said as I entered the kitchen, "I've got to ask you something. Are we supposed to be here for dinner?"

"Yes," he responded brightly, but then added, "I just heard about it." That lacked certain clarity.

"Did you just find out about it three days ago or three minutes ago?" Much to our relief, his answer was days ago. "Go on in," he continued, "they're expecting you."

We walked through the dining room and on into the living room where President and Mrs. Bush saw us coming, put down their books, rose from their chairs and greeted us warmly, "Tom, Shirley, welcome!"

Come to find out, we learned through the course of the evening that during the Labor Day weekend the president had decided to have a few guests over. In keeping with family tradition, they had

95

stayed home over the holiday so that as many of those around him could be with their families. With no staff around, he had made the calls himself. He had told Ariel of his plans but had forgotten to call the gate to let them know that we were coming. Not long after, three more couples arrived, including Brent Scowcroft, Lenier and Karla Temerlin, and Dan and Harriet Burke.

It was a wonderful evening, filled with easy, pleasant conversation, fascinating subject matter and good cheer. The president talked of the aircraft carrier that was being built in his name and donned for our pleasure a presidential version of a country music jacket that had been given to him by the *Oak Ridge Boys*.

As we drove home that night all of our early apprehensions had been long forgotten. We felt blessed to be in George and Barbara Bush's circle of friends. That circle is a wide one, we realized, as large and varying as the backgrounds, resources and interests of the nation they have spent their lifetime serving.

"Yes," we said once again, "we are blessed."

Tom & Shirley Bradbury

F U N

HUMOR

In June of '93, the year President Bush left office, I was invited to lunch at Walker's Point. President Bush had been out of office only five months.

I arrived at the house on a beautiful bluebird Maine day and went out to the deck by the sea where a table with an umbrella was set up. President Bush and another gentleman were out there. Mrs. Bush hadn't arrived yet. The president introduced me to his friend and ushered me in to sit down.

"Would you like some wine," he said eagerly.

"Sure," I replied, and he started pouring. I was feeling a bit nervous so I politely paused before drinking until President Bush, still holding the wine bottle, looked at me and said, "Well, aren't you going to taste it?"

I took a sip and turned to speak with the other gentleman. Wine bottle still in hand, the president looked eagerly at me and said, "Well, what do you think?"

"It's very good," I said.

A big grin creased his face as he said proudly, "I got it by the case at *Sam's Club*."

He was so excited about being able to go to a big box store and buy what he wanted at a great price.

It was Kendall Jackson Reserve Chardonnay and I've had a soft spot in my heart for it ever since.

Susan Biddle

Sometime around the summer of 2000, my wife Nancy and I received an invitation from Barbara and George Bush to come to their home on Walker's Point to hear the Yale Glee Club. We joined a number of other guests in their living room for cocktails and an informal performance. The student leader of the glee club made a few remarks and noted that President Bush had been made an honorary member of the club and, in accordance with their custom, he was given a nickname, "ferme' la bouche", which translates roughly to "close your mouth."

He accepted the nickname with his customary good humor.

Dick Thigpen

One Sunday morning in the fall, I spotted the Bushes on the beach at Goose Rocks, which is a short drive north of their home at Walker's Point. Mrs. Bush was obviously intensely focused on searching for specific shells. The President seemed to be attempting to help but Barbara just kept shaking her head "no" every time he showed her something he had picked up. Finally, in apparent frustration, he slammed the contents of his hand to the sand and threw his hands in the air. I felt that I had observed the Bushes in a very candid and private moment.

Linda Rice

On one of my visits to Walker's Point, President Bush decided we needed to go parasailing. Of course, everyone was all excited but I don't do heights. So, I was designated to be the official photographer for the adventure. I thought I was safe. Of course, I ended up being shamed into going by the president, who was always a bit mischievous. Once I somewhat reluctantly agreed to give it a go, the guy running the parasail explained that I could give him a signal and he would stop my climb. I was somewhat reassured but not confident. In theory, this was great, except every time I gave the signal I could hear the president tell the guy, "higher, higher!"

When I finally got back on the boat I was noodles. It is a great memory of a wonderful day spent with President Bush.

Donna Sterban

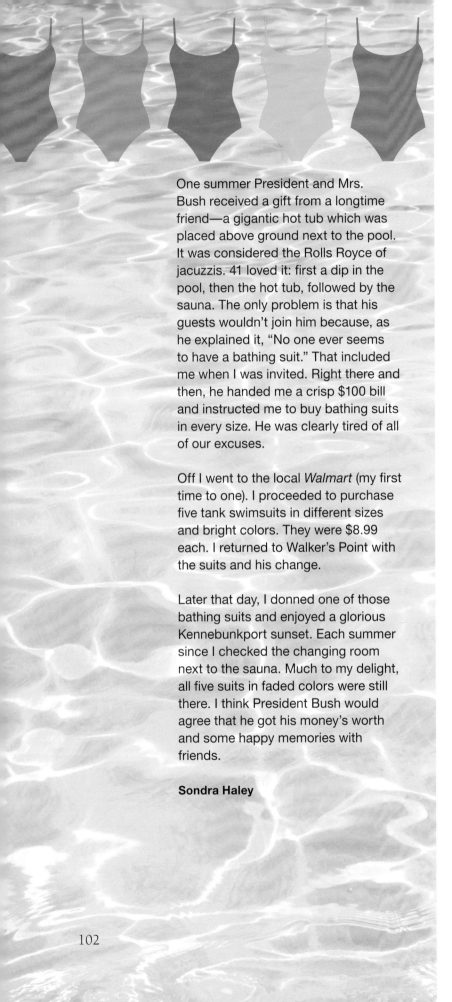

One summer President and Mrs. Bush received a gift from a longtime friend—a gigantic hot tub which was placed above ground next to the pool. It was considered the Rolls Royce of jacuzzis. 41 loved it: first a dip in the pool, then the hot tub, followed by the sauna. The only problem is that his guests wouldn't join him because, as he explained it, "No one ever seems to have a bathing suit." That included me when I was invited. Right there and then, he handed me a crisp $100 bill and instructed me to buy bathing suits in every size. He was clearly tired of all of our excuses.

Off I went to the local *Walmart* (my first time to one). I proceeded to purchase five tank swimsuits in different sizes and bright colors. They were $8.99 each. I returned to Walker's Point with the suits and his change.

Later that day, I donned one of those bathing suits and enjoyed a glorious Kennebunkport sunset. Each summer since I checked the changing room next to the sauna. Much to my delight, all five suits in faded colors were still there. I think President Bush would agree that he got his money's worth and some happy memories with friends.

Sondra Haley

My wife Dottie and I decided to give a significant donation to the Kennebunkport Conservation Trust, one of the local land trusts and a particular favorite of President Bush. We drove over to the Trust headquarters to give our check to Tom Bradbury, the executive director. We asked him to make sure our gift remained anonymous.

The next day, I played golf at the Cape Arundel Golf Club, which was frequented by the president. I had just hit a good tee shot on the 6th hole, across the pond, and onto the green. Suddenly, Ken Raynor, the Club golf pro at the time, drives up in a golf cart with President Bush. The president hops out of the cart and says, "Bob, that is such a great gift you gave to the Trust!"

Startled, I said, "How the heck did you know about that?"

Without hesitation, he said "I was head of the CIA, you know!"

Bob King

RANKING COMMITTEE
JUNE 8, 2000

In honor of Barbara Bush's 75th birthday, which was celebrated with family and friends at The River Club, President Bush decided to reveal for the first time the members of the top-secret family "ranking committee." For years this committee had ranked family members on everything from the jokes they told to their tennis and horseshoe game. The rules were very elaborate and strict and often determined who in the family could challenge other family members to a contest. The photo "reveal" confirmed what most of the family had suspected for years: This was a committee of one.

Jean Becker
Chief of Staff to George H.W. Bush
1994-2018

President George H. W. Bush was a giant of a man, both literally and figuratively. When seated, President Bush sat as tall as me at my full height: 5'3". On the domestic and international stage, President Bush was also a giant—a larger-than-life icon of The Greatest Generation. One might think that to be in the presence of such a senior statesman would be an intimidating experience, but quite the opposite was true. President Bush was genuinely kind, gentle, humble and most of all funny. His humor and gentlemanly demeanor put you at ease immediately.

My favorite President Bush story happened shortly after June 12, 2014, his 90th birthday. In conjunction with my responsibilities for planning Kennebunkport Historical Society festivities and exhibits to celebrate his birthday, I had occasion to visit Walker's Point a few times around his birthday. On one trip I had the opportunity to sit down and chat with him in his office.

The president talked about his birthday and how overwhelmed he had been with the outpouring of love from so many people. Most of all, we talked about how excited he was to have jumped out of a plane on his 90th birthday.

For the Historical Society's commemorative exhibit at Kennebunkport's First Families Museum to celebrate his 90th birthday, he was generously lending the jumpsuit he had worn. He joked about the message he had had embroidered on the back collar, a classic example of his humor. Only one person would see that message—Mike Elliott, the former Golden Knight Paratrooper with whom he jumped tandem that morning. The message read simply: "Pay Attention."

It was a great morning, and I have the treasured memento of a photo taken of me with the president.

About a month later, I took my daughter Gillian to a matinee at the Arundel Barn Playhouse for an annual mother/daughter outing. Just as we sat down, President and Mrs. Bush came in through a side door to take their front row seats. As was usual, the crowd gave a standing ovation. The President and Mrs. Bush waved graciously and took their seats.

At intermission, my daughter strolled over to Mrs. Bush. The next thing I know Mrs. Bush is waving for me to come over and get in the picture of her, my daughter and the president. As I joined them, an observant Secret Service agent, with a wry smile of humor, shouted, "Weren't you wearing the same dress the last time I took your picture?" I turned three shades of red. Sensing my embarrassment, the president took my hand and whispered in my ear, "It's a good thing I changed my shirt." He said it just loud enough to get a laugh and an "Oh, George!" from Mrs. Bush.

Kirsten Camp

One summer at Walker's Point, I happened to be at the right— or wrong— place. President Bush was known for spontaneously inviting folks out on his beloved boat. I was the beneficiary of his benevolent invites many times. As many experienced, he loved to thrill his guests with speed. I knew to hold on tight and secure my hair.

This particular *Fidelity* jaunt was with a lovely couple from Houston. Off the four of us went fast and furious. Then we stopped and the fishing poles came out. I had never just sat still, bobbing on the water. Uh oh… this isn't good…I get motion sickness.

Discreetly I made my way to the bow taking deep breaths and looking out

on the horizon. Soon after, I threw up over the side of the boat. I was trying to pretend all was fine when I felt President Bush at my side. He handed me a tissue and said, "Welcome to the club. I once threw up on the Prime Minister of Japan."

Sondra Haley

When I was operating my sightseeing boat, *Elizabeth II*, in the Kennebunk River, President Bush decided to go fishing in the basin to the north of the bridge that separates Kennebunk from Kennebunkport. It is a very low bridge, even at the lowest tide…and this excursion was on an outgoing tide. President Bush made it under the bridge and happily continued fishing. The Secret Service boat couldn't clear the space beneath the bridge due to the high radar arch they had in the center of the boat. To keep up with him, the Secret Service team started to disassemble the arch while a Navy Seal attired in a wet suit climbed up on the bridge with binoculars. Finally, they completed the disassembly of the arch and went under the bridge—just as 41 decided to turn and come back under. He passed by us with a grin on his face.

Wayne Showalter

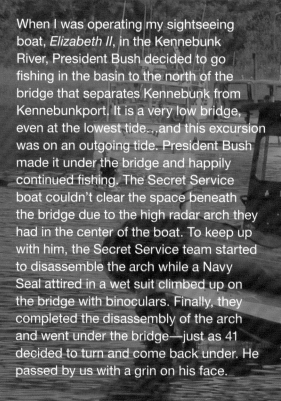

One day I went to *Marden's* in Sanford, a local surplus and salvage store, and found a caricature slipper of George Bush in a big wooden crate. I thought that perhaps a similar slipper for Barbara might be in there too, so I continued to rummage through the selection. And there it was, a Barbara Bush caricature slipper! The slippers were a result of the famous picture of them in bed at Walker's Point with their grandchildren surrounding them. I brought these treasures to the President's retirement gathering on the Village Green in Kennebunkport and asked President Bush if he would sign his slipper. He happily obliged. When Barbara came along, I asked her to sign her slipper as well. She rolled her eyes and hesitated. When I said that the president had signed, she too signed a slipper. I was the happiest young Republican at that moment. They will be missed.

Kristin Blomberg

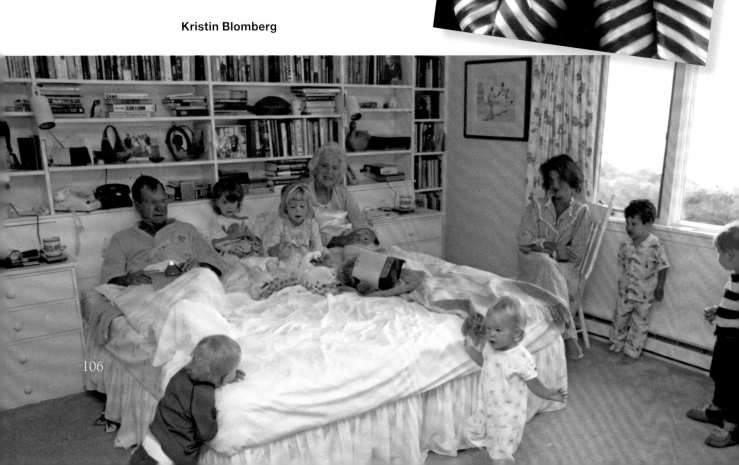

An obvious photo choice for a story about President Bush might have been of the two us on his beloved speedboat *Fidelity.* How lucky am I that I have a huge collection of these photos, going to lunch at *Barnacle Billy's* in Ogunquit, or out to find whales or visit the seals, jumping big waves or fishing in still water. Or a lot of times, just racing around for the love of racing around. Many of these photos are quite dramatic, with me wearing Hollywood-style sunglasses and our hair blowing gloriously in the wind.

Yet, this was the photo that spoke to my heart. It's the photo that I think reveals the most about George Herbert Walker Bush: He was fun. He was a lot of fun. He was the champion of unexpected fun.

He made all our lives joyful.

So how to explain the photo above, where he appears to be wearing an aardvark hat. Wait, it IS an aardvark hat.

Maybe I should explain that President Bush was also the biggest idea man I have ever met. I sometimes lived in fear of when he said, "Jean, I have an idea." Sometimes it would be something simple like, "Let's go to lunch on the boat." But other times it would be something a tad bigger, like "I am going to start jumping out of perfectly good airplanes."

On this particular day, he decided to interview everyone on Walker's Point about what we loved about life in Maine, and then bury the VHS tape in a time capsule on Walker's Point. (Yes, it's still there.)

What we didn't expect was for him to conduct all the interviews wearing an aardvark hat.

Why, you might ask? It was fun. It was different. It was an icebreaker.

So he spent the day in his makeshift studio in the yard down by the office, interviewing everyone from their longtime housekeeper Paula Rendon to his son, the 43rd President of the United States. And he never took the hat off.

Joyful.

Jean Becker
*Chief of Staff to George H.W. Bush
1994-2018*

KINDNESS

I have known President and Mrs. Bush since his presidency. To say they have inspired me is an understatement. Over the years I have spent time with them in a variety of locations, but none was more special than Kennebunkport. Aside from attending the Barbara Bush Foundation for Family Literacy's "Maine Celebration of Reading," and taking part in the festivities surrounding Mrs. Bush's 90th birthday, among the most memorable experiences were the two times that 41 hosted a group of wounded warriors at Walker's Point.

The occasion was the launch of two of my books, both focusing on wounded warriors, their caregivers and the animals that help them heal. President Bush wanted to meet all of them and despite not feeling well, he insisted on having his personal aide wheel him down the long driveway so he could personally shake each of the wounded warriors' hands. It was a magical moment for the veterans and clearly for the president as well. Before each event, I had a chance to sit with him and brief him on the visit. He was so happy to be able to host these heroes despite not feeling his best.

After the first visit, one of the wounded warriors—U.S. Army Specialist Tyler Jeffries (RET.)—was planning to get engaged afterwards at *David's*, one of the local restaurants. When 43 and 41 heard about the plan they insisted that Tyler call his girlfriend, Lauren, who was shopping in town, and have her come over to Walker's Point ASAP. They wanted Tyler to propose in front of both presidents and first ladies as well as the other wounded warriors and their mothers. Luckily, Lauren said yes!

The next group of wounded warriors came to Walker's Point two years later along with a variety of animals that help them deal with physical tasks and emotional support. They included service dogs, a potbelly pig and two wounded screech owls. President Bush loved meeting them all. But when one of the wounded warriors brought an owl over to meet the president, the owl had a massive accident that landed right on 41's pants. The veteran was humiliated and upset. President Bush laughed, and Mrs. Bush told them not to worry because 41 had plenty of other pants in the house.

These visits were life changing for all of the wounded warriors and their mothers who had the honor of meeting 41 and Mrs. Bush in Kennebunkport. They will forever cherish those moments in Maine and will never forget the generosity of the 41st President of the United States.

Dava Guerin

President Bush was the epitome of kindness and master of the small gesture. He seemed to recognize that meeting a president was not an every day experience for most people. He always took the time to greet people warmly, appear in a photo or shake a hand to acknowledge anyone who approached him. Recognizing that many people were too shy to ask for a photo, he often would ask if they wanted a photo with him. He particularly seemed to appreciate those who dedicated their lives to the service of others.

Early in his presidency, he was kind enough to reach out to a woman who was an outstanding point of light in her community. While it was small gesture from his perspective, the story became a sensation in her hometown.

Always dressed in her white nursing uniform and cap, just as she had for a remarkable 61 years, Dorothy "Dot" Woodbury, RN, 78, was a deeply respected fixture at Henrietta D. Goodall Hospital

in Sanford, Maine—a small local hospital 18 miles west of Kennebunkport. When a colleague, Elaine Guillemette, RN, contacted the White House with the hope of surprising Dot with a special letter recognizing her six decades of service, she received far more; what she got was typically George Bush.

Shortly after sending the letter in January 1989, Elaine fielded a call from the White House inviting Dot to meet the president. Stunned, Elaine was asked to keep the plans quiet until all could be confirmed and a date set. In early August, Elaine received final word that the meeting was to occur when the president arrived home that month for his summer vacation in Kennebunkport.

Elaine broke the news to Dot a day before the planned meeting. Dot sat for a moment with her mouth agape, not quite believing what she had heard. After all, she had never seen, much less met, a President of the United States. The president, however, was clearly intrigued by the story of her career.

Dot graduated from Sanford High School in 1928, the same year that the hospital where she would spend her life was founded. She began her training to be a nurse at the H.D. Goodall Hospital School of Nursing, only blocks from where she grew up. For over six decades this remarkable woman, who physically didn't top the five foot mark but whose heart was as big as all outdoors, dedicated her life to caring for the people of her mill town community. Through the Depression, World War II, and the closing of most of the massive Sanford mills in the 1950s, Dot stood by, delivering babies, working as an anesthetist, recruiting nurses and, at one point, even running the hospital. There was likely not a task there that she had not performed. She had no children of her own; the community was her family.

In an interview with her many years ago, I recall asking her what time she arrived at work. She paused for a moment, looked me square in the eye and said, "I don't go to work, I report for duty." As a nurse, she knew the value of professionalism and dedication, which is why she always appeared in a freshly pressed clean white nursing outfit with white stockings and white shoes, all topped with the crisp white nursing cap that she received as a graduate of the H.D. Goodall Hospital School of Nursing. This was her uniform; nursing was her calling.

By the time the invitation to meet the president arrived, Dot was nearing 80 and, despite a visible limp left over from a childhood illness, she reported for duty early every day, uniform freshly pressed, shoes glowing white and a smile ready to greet colleagues and patients alike. The hospital leadership, in a nod of respect toward her advanced age and uncommon service record, provided her with a position as a pharmacy technician where the hours were predictable, the stress level low and the physical requirements minimal.

On the appointed day, Dot was escorted to Pease Air Force Base in Portsmouth, New Hampshire where she was to greet the president as he deplaned from Air Force One. As President Bush appeared at the plane doorway, the crowd, in-cluding a busload of Goodall Hospital employees on hand for the occasion, cheered loudly. Dot, who had chosen to wear her white nursing uniform, glowed brightly in the midsummer sun. The president greeted her warmly at the base of the stairs, sharing a few brief comments and smiling broadly. Afterward, as he walked across the tarmac toward the marine helicopter, he paused, turned toward Dot, and gave her his famous thumbs up sign, a fitting tribute to a nursing career that spanned the tenures of 11 U.S. presidents starting with Calvin Coolidge.

Afterward, as Dot stood surrounded by reporters and photographers, she clasped her hands and raised them proudly above her head. It felt good to be recognized by a kindred spirit who shared her dedication to public service.

Dot remained at Goodall Hospital for 65 years before retiring, eventually having a building there, which once housed the nursing school where she began her career, named in her honor.

Tim Dietz

In August of 2010, after a particularly enjoyable afternoon of boating, we returned to the Marblehead launching ramp on the Saco River to haul our boat out. As we tied to the dock, we realized that President Bush was sitting in his brand new *Fidelity V* on the other side of the dock with his daughter Doro and some others. The folks from Fountain Powerboats had just trailered the new boat up from North Carolina and his old *Fidelity IV* was now sitting on the trailer up in the parking lot waiting to go back south.

I'm an avid boater, so I struck up a conversation with the president about his new boat and the three 300HP engines that it sported! He enjoyed talking about the boat and we had a nice conversation.

Then I mentioned to him that we had plans to go out to dinner at *Nunan's Lobster Hut* that night with someone I thought he knew— a world-renowned orthopedic surgeon who lives near Walker's Point. The surgeon had mentored my daughter in a fellowship at Columbia. In fact, he and the president have apparently been friends for years.

When I mentioned the doctor's name to the president, he responded quickly saying "Now HE's the important person, not me." I learned that it was President Bush's style not to seek accolades but to deflect accolades to others. And to hear that coming from a man who was once the most powerful person in the world was moving.

There was another time in the early '90s while he was in office, when, while out on a fishing expedition in an earlier *Fidelity*, his boat began smoking badly. The Secret Service raced over to see what was happening and discovered that it was just a broken cooling hose spraying steam. It was, of course, picked up by the media and was big news for a day or two.

At the time, I just happened to be trying to sell a 27 foot Boston Whaler and I figured why not? I sent a letter and some photos to President Bush at the White House explaining that my boat might be a good alternative to the boat he had. I figured that I could always tell a good story about having written to the president. It got even better when he responded. He didn't want the boat, but he was such a gentleman in taking the time to respond. He even complimented my boat.

Jim Boselli

It is very humbling and a great honor to have the opportunity to share a few thoughts and stories about the very special friendship I enjoyed with my fishing buddy, President George H.W. Bush.

At the beginning, I want to give thanks to our Creator for the many blessings he has given me in my life. My sisters and I were immensely blessed to always have the steadfast support and unconditional love of our mom and dad, John A. and Genny Morris. Having spent the majority of my life observing my dad in all types of situations I can honestly say that, as a son, I admired and respected my dad more than any man I have ever known. He was, plain and simple, my hero and I loved him more than I can ever say.

After my dad passed, for over 30 years I had the wonderful, good fortune to spend countless personal hours and days with another wonderful man, President George H.W. Bush. During our time together, I came to develop the same immense level of admiration and respect for President Bush as I had held for my father, I truly loved him like a second dad. I often pinch myself when I think about how a hillbilly from the Missouri Ozarks could have the incredible good fortune to become such close, personal friends with this special man, the 41st President of the United States.

When I think of our friendship, I'm reminded of my favorite quote from Ernest Hemingway: "In a life spent fishing I've come to realize it's not the big fish you catch, but the people you meet, the friends that you make along the way that matter the most."

President Bush and I became close friends through our shared love of fishing

and by working together to enhance the future of fishing through conservation. You really get to know a fellow well when you're fishing and sharing time together in a boat or wading side by side in a pristine, free-flowing stream or sitting around a peaceful campfire in a remote tent camp.

The man I got to know in these peaceful times was the most thoughtful, kindhearted, down-to-earth, humble, family-loving soul you could ever imagine. Among the most treasured times in my life were the many fishing adventure trips shared with President Bush, his young grandson "Jebby" and Kennebunkport golf professional, and our great friend, Ken Raynor.

Together we fished in some of the most remote and beautiful rivers in the world from Tree River above the Arctic Circle in the Northwest Territories for Arctic Char; to The River Test in England (considered the birthplace of fly-fishing) for Trout; to the majestic Atlantic Salmon Rivers in Newfoundland and Labrador; to the Florida Keys for Tarpon and Bonefish; to bass lakes in Alabama and to Dogwood Canyon Creek and Table Rock Lake in my home state of Missouri.

Yes, the president loved to fish! He really, really, really loved to fish. He loved to be on the water, he would stay out there all day if he could, and there could be no doubt that although he had the good fortune to fish around the world, the coast of Maine, off Kennebunkport, was the

"In a life spent fishing I've come to realize it's not the big fish you catch, but the people you meet, the friends that you make along the way that matter the most."

Ernest Hemingway

place above all others that called to his heart.

He especially loved casting, fly-fishing mainly. He was a lefty, and he was a beautiful fly caster. He was so passionate about it. I remember, the president used to have these cleats that he would put on his shoes, and he'd climb up and down the big rocks and boulders at his home in Kennebunkport. It was slippery; the ocean rocks had seaweed and moss all over them. But he loved to cast right off the shoreline. The Secret Service would have to go with him, and it was funny to me to see how they'd grit their teeth, as if to say, "Oh boy, we've got to do this again!"

He also loved his fishing boat *Fidelity*. It was pretty much a speedboat that he would fish from and hotrod around in. The president's fishing exploits would often provide an added challenge for his

Secret Service detail, following along in their inflatable Zodiac boats. One time we were in *Fidelity* and he said, "Johnny, watch this," as he sped up the boat, the Secret Service had to try and keep up. He always had a little kid in him.

When we were fishing, we almost never talked about politics. We talked about the joys of fishing and the fun things in life. We talked about worries and challenges from time to time. Mostly we talked about family. The president was deeply devoted to his family. One of the joys of my life was seeing the president fishing with his grandson, Jebby.

Of course, sometimes politics could not be avoided. One time we were in Kennebunkport fishing for stripers and bluefish, and the Secret Service man in the boat said, "Mr. President, we must return to the mainland for you to take an urgent call on a secure line." It was the leader of the Soviet Union, Mikhail Gorbachev; he had just been held in an attempted coup. After he got free, the first world leader he called was President Bush, a man he held in the highest personal regard.

So that was just a little bit of unexpected history and made me realize the magnitude and responsibilities carried by my fishing buddy.

There is another, even more amazing, "close call" story. This time the Secret Service agents actually saved the president's life. It took place in the summer of 1995. We were the guests of our great friends Craig and Elaine Dobbins from Newfoundland. Craig loved fly-fishing and was a committed conservationist. As CEO of Canadian

Helicopter, he made access to remote rivers available to us with his aircraft.

One particular morning, as we were flying off to fish the beautiful Hawk River it got too foggy and we had to land. As soon as we did, the president went off into a wooded area to relieve himself. The Secret Service agents stayed a respectful distance behind, but after what seemed like a very long time they went to look for him. It turned out he had wandered into a bog and was up to his armpits in quicksand. Talk about a startling sight! Fortunately, the president, as he often did, remained calm and instead of thrashing around in a panic, which would have caused the bog to suck him completely under, he stayed still with

his arms outspread, trusting he would be found. It was a tricky situation and rescuing him from that quicksand was not easy considering he was already in it up to his neck.

To this day, I don't believe many people including his closest friends, and even his family, realize what a very, very close call this was, how close we came to losing him in the quicksand.

Our Conservation President

There is something else I believe very few people realize: President Bush was a deeply committed conservationist. In the end, I believe it was the president's own unassuming humility that deprived him of some of the recognition he so

deserves for what he did for conservation and the environment. Hopefully history and future generations will come to more fully celebrate his many remarkable contributions.

While the president and I didn't discuss politics, we did discuss conservation. He was always probing everyone about how the government could and should be involved in protecting the air, water and wilderness. And it was inevitable that his deep devotion to the sport and the environment would find its way into his profession. He brought his love of fishing and the outdoors to the White House with him. His passion for conservation was reflected in legislation like the Clean Water Act and by various protections of the wetlands and much more.

A classic example was his "Fisherman's Intercom Committee." He would invite his fishing buddies to come to meetings at the White House with the Secretary of the Interior and the Director of the U.S. Fish and Wildlife Service. He would say, "I want my fishing buddies to speak up and tell us what we need to do better." He was that passionate about fishing, and the development of fishing resources was a great priority in his life and work.

In 2014, President Bush received the inaugural Keep America Fishing Lifetime Achievement Award for his lifelong personal commitment to recreational fishing and conservation of America's fisheries and wetlands. The award was well deserved.

I'm proud to highlight some of his other extraordinary conservation achievements: As vice president, he played a key role in the passage of the Wallop-

121

Breaux amendments to the Sport Fish Restoration Act, which generates more than $650 million per year for sport fish restoration, access, and other fishing and boating projects. During his term as president, he established the first national policy goal of "no net loss" of wetlands. Remarkably, he established 56 new wildlife refuges, more than any other president including President Roosevelt, restored three million acres of wetlands, and signed the Clean Air Act reauthorization that required cleaner burning fuels. These common-sense policies moved forward because he took the time to become informed on conservation issues of the day, and because he had the passion, foresight and ability to build a consensus on all sides, including both sides of the aisle. Many feel that his signature achievement was the Americans with Disabilities Act, which he signed into law in 1990. Among the great things it made possible for Americans with disabilities, I especially celebrate the fact that it gave many of these individuals access to the outdoors and outdoor activities not previously available to them.

I know this little remembrance is about George Bush the man, but it is important to say that he lived his principles and changed our country for the better forever.

One of the great honors of my life was speaking on behalf of the president upon his induction into the Bass Fishing Hall of Fame in 2016. His health was fading, and he could not make it, but he sent a beautiful letter about his love of fishing

that he asked me to read. I think about that letter often. The president talked about his humble beginning, as a young angler fishing on the cold waters along the coast of Maine using nothing more than a lead jig and a piece of white cloth for bait. He never forgot those days, never forgot—even after he became President of the United States—where he began. And he concluded with these words that I still hold dear:

"There's a lesson here I want to share with you. Whatever you love to do— whether it's fishing, hiking, hunting or kayaking—hold on to it. As you pursue success in school, and later in your careers, don't forget to find time for the things you love to do. If you stay true to the hobbies of your youth, you will find a source of relaxation and replenishment that will never fail you."

Sometimes, when we were out fishing together, I would ask myself, "How did I get so lucky in my life to become friends with such a wonderful, genuine man?" I thank God for President Bush and the great joys of fishing that brought us together.

Johnny Morris
Founder, Bass Pro Shops

*A meeting of the Fisherman's
Intercom Committee in the
Oval Office*

123

The man I got to know in these peaceful times was the most thoughtful, kindhearted, down-to-earth, humble, family-loving soul you could ever imagine.

ME 8088 H

As a long time summer resident of Kennebunkport, I met President Bush many times. Whether at the Cape Arundel Golf Course, in a local restaurant, or spotting him fishing off Timber Island, he was always in a good mood and friendly. He personally thanked us each time we let him play through on the golf course.

My favorite story happened at the Kennebunk River Club where we were all watching a foursome of retired Australian tennis pros put on an exhibition match. Sitting on the deck overlooking Court One I was seated one person to the right of President Bush. It was getting late in the afternoon and the mosquitoes started to appear. He applied some bug spray and leaned over to me and asked if I would like some. I was so taken by his offer that I accepted, even though I don't usually use repellant. His small gesture exemplifies what a kind and sharing person we all knew him to be throughout his life. I will always remember that moment with fondness.

Clancy Cottman

We were concluding a meeting with a specialist at Maine Medical Center's Barbara Bush Children's Hospital, discussing my daughter's prognosis and treatment plan for cancer. There was knock on the door. A nurse poked her head in and said that we had some special visitors. When the door opened wide, there was my daughter Kayla, sitting in the company of George H.W. Bush and his wife Barbara. I was a little overwhelmed.

At the time I didn't know that they had lost a daughter, Robin, to cancer many years before. They spent a fair amount of time with us, which gave my daughter a much-needed boost. She talked about her special visitors for many days afterward.

A few days later, I was called downstairs to the restaurant that we lived above at the time. Mrs. Bush and several of her grandchildren were seated for lunch. When we saw her in the hospital, my hair had been long, well below my shoulders. I had since had it cut short. Mrs. Bush seemed to like my new look.

I will hold dear to the special memories of the kindness of President and Mrs. Bush, who continued to visit the Barbara Bush Children's Hospital until her passing. They will never know how much their visit meant to us.

Marc Cote

My daughter Kayla had bone cancer. In 2001, on her 14th birthday, the President and Mrs. Bush came to visit her in the hospital. She died not long after the visit. It meant so much to her and to our family and always will.

Julia Brennan

As a young man, long before he became internationally known, President Bush was as considerate and helpful as he was throughout his remarkable life of service to others.

In the 1960's my sister, Janet Jones, and I, with our two small sons, were in a sailboat with an outboard motor cruising on the Kennebunk River and heading to the ocean when our propeller got tangled with a rope from a buoy. We were stuck and did not know what to do when future President 41 came by in his boat, saw that we were in distress and asked if he could help. I replied with a grateful "Yes." He took off his watch, grabbed a knife, and jumped into the river to cut the line and free our small sailboat. With a smile and a pleasant admonition "to be careful", he was on his way.

As a young man, long before he became internationally known, President Bush was as considerate and helpful as he was throughout his remarkable life of service to others.

Nancy Shand Thigpen

We had the good fortune to be guests of Carol and Bert Walker at their place in Kennebunkport over the Fourth of July. We had an incredible opportunity to spend the holidays with the extended Bush family. We were struck by their humility, kindness, lack of airs, wit, and patriotism. I had the chance to greet 41 and I told him that I was grateful to meet him and I thanked him for his service. I also told him that he was the greatest president of my lifetime. He winked and said, "Well, that's because you're so young." I was 55!

What an experience! What a hero and a gentleman.

Martha Schlicher

President Bush was a kind, thoughtful person who was constantly doing things for other people.

I spent five summers in Kennebunkport as Mrs. Bush's aide and grew to love the area. So when my husband and I got engaged several years after I left their employ, we decided that we would have a destination wedding in Kennebunkport with a few close friends and family. I went on the hunt for the right location for a wedding reception and found several good options. However, one day President Bush called me and insisted that we hold the reception at Walker's Point.

I have many, many special memories of President and Mrs. Bush and Kennebunkport, but my wedding day spent at their home is one that my family, friends, and my husband JT and I will certainly never forget.

Quincy Crawford

We used to be co-owners of the local village market where the Bushes did much of their shopping during the summer season. One year, we were invited to attend a small reception at Walker's Point. After a pleasant time of socializing, all were invited to go up by the pool to be entertained by Yale's a cappella singing group, *the Whiffenpoofs*. Chairs had been set up by the pool but all seats were taken by the time we arrived, so my husband and I stood contentedly in the back. President and Mrs. Bush were the last to take their places in the front row. As the president was beginning to sit he glanced back and saw us standing. "How un-gallant," he stated as he rose and headed our way. He took my arm and led me to his seat saying, "Shirley, you sit here with Barbara. I'll stand up back with Tom and negotiate food prices." What a gentleman!

Shirley Bradbury

During the presidential years I served as a local volunteer driver for the president. I was called on from time to time to pick up guests, drive in motorcades and the like. One day I was at Walker's Point while President Bush was filming a commercial for Coast Guard safety. The film crew shot take after take of the president as he stood on the stone pier at the compound. It didn't seem like things were going as smoothly as was hoped.

During one break, several of the Bush grandchildren approached the president. He bent down and they whispered in his ear. Suddenly, the president turned and jumped fully clothed off the dock and into the water. A fully dressed Navy Seal, reacting to what he thought might be an emergency, dove in after him. President Bush surfaced, swam a few strokes back to the pier and hauled himself dripping wet onto the dock. The grandkids ran up to him laughing and said, "We didn't think that you'd do it!"

"Pay up," said the president with apparent delight. The children dug through their pockets and gave him all they had.

Barbara Bush, who had witnessed all of this, approached the laughing crew, not looking all that amused. She wanted to know what the shenanigans were all about. "I won a dollar forty-seven cents," replied the president, showing her the money in his hand.

Barbara looked at the change then looked up at the president with steely eyes and scolded him.

"Do you see that man over there?" she said, pointing at the Navy Seal who was now standing on the dock, his clothes soaking wet. "He's probably been polishing those boots all day because he was going to be near the president. Now you've made him go in after you!"

President Bush started to reply that it was essentially that man's job to do that and it wasn't that big a deal but Barbara wouldn't hear of it.

"You owe him an apology," she declared. And so, looking somewhat sheepish, President Bush went over to apologize, apparently to the delight of the Navy Seal who said that it was no problem at all.

From all that I witnessed over the years, this sort of thoughtful response was not unusual. The Bushes really cared about those around them and always looked out for the comfort and safety of family, friends and presidential staff.

Steve Adams

I first visited Kennebunkport in August 1992 after reading in the USA Today about President Bush's vacation the previous summer. After several summers of seeing photos of the president seemingly in every restaurant and store in Kennebunkport, I realized I was never in the right place at the right time. So I wrote President Bush a lighthearted letter in 2000 saying something like "You seem to have met every person in Kennebunkport. How does one go about meeting a president?"

In response, I received a personal letter from the president that still makes me laugh to this day.

Dear Tricia,

I am sorry to have proved such an elusive target all these years.

You asked how one might run into me here in Kennebunkport. Well, the truth is, Tricia, I hardly know myself. Much as Bar and I would love to spend every day here at Walker's Point, our family and friends frequently have other plans for us.

When I am here, you'll have to ask the fish who swim off the Point when and how to run into me, because they do it far more often than they would like, I am sure.

Perhaps next summer will be your lucky summer!

Your friend,
George Bush

I can't believe I had the nerve to write such a letter. And how did I get so lucky to get a response? His final sentence turned out to be a prophecy because two summers later I got my long-awaited picture with the president.

On July 17, 2002, we were staying at the old *Schooner's Inn* on Ocean Avenue. I saw President Bush bringing his boat *Fidelity* into the Kennebunk River followed closely by the Secret Service boat. Knowing that the president often stopped at the marina down the street I figured I'd take a chance and walk down. He had to get off the boat sometime, right?

As I was passing the *Yachtsman Motel*, I saw a buzz of activity. As I got closer I realized that the president had docked *Fidelity* and a crowd was waiting to greet him. Completely star struck, I handed my camera to some random stranger who had just gotten her picture taken with the president.

I didn't manage to do much but smile and utter a "Thanks!" as the president graciously waited for the photo to be taken.

This was before I had a digital camera, so the most nerve-racking part was waiting a few days until I got home and could get the photo developed. I feared I had my eyes closed or the picture would be blurry or my spur-of-the-moment photographer had cut the top of the president's head off.

Much to my relief, the picture was perfect. It is proudly framed in my home and is now one of my favorite Facebook profile pictures.

Our annual trips to Maine won't be quite the same. We can no longer look for *Fidelity* in the river or visit *Mabel's Lobster Claw* with the hope that President and Mrs. Bush will stop in. But, I am grateful that the president not only docked his boat that morning in 2002 but also introduced me—however indirectly—to a place called Kennebunkport.

Tricia Gorman

FOR A GOOD CAUSE

President George H.W. Bush was a generous and giving man who truly lived his points of light philosophy. On a local level, he and Mrs. Bush were often co-chairs for capital campaigns to support many good causes in southern Maine from Kennebunk's Brick Store Museum, the Kennebunkport Conservation Trust, Kennebunkport's Louis T. Graves Memorial Public Library or the Kennebunkport Historical Society's First Families Museum to the University of New England and major medical centers in the southern Maine region, including Southern Maine Health Care, Maine Medical Center and Mercy Hospital. They not only gave their names but their time, effort and financial support. There are countless organizations that will miss their kindness, generosity and willingness to step forward and lead.

Dorothy Walker Bush A life of Inspiration

Southern Maine Medical Center

DOROTHY WALKER BUSH PAVILION

I lived with the former president. Well, maybe not WITH him, but close enough. My home is in Kennebunk, right across the river from Kennebunkport. Should you follow American politics with more than a passing interest you know that Kennebunkport was the summer home of George H.W. Bush, the 41st President of the United States.

For just about 40 years, before his passing in 2018, we were practically neighbors. Well, almost anyway. He lived in a sprawling estate on Walker's Point, a spectacular peninsula that cuts a rocky swath deep into the North Atlantic. For most of my our time in Maine, we lived about two miles away in a 200 year-old home built by a guy who made cabinets for wooden sailing ships, which gives you a pretty good idea of its relative size. We now live in a new house we built next door. I tell folks that we've gone upscale and moved about a hundred feet closer to the beach, which is still about a mile and a half away.

Thousands of tourists have long since discovered that you can get a great view of the Bush estate from Ocean Avenue, a narrow road that meanders along seaside cliffs past seasonal cottages large enough to be hotels. Most people would call them mansions. On this side of the river, few tourists frequent our street, even though this old road has seen more than its share of history.

Locations and stations aside, the former president and I had two things in common: We called the Kennebunks home and neither one of us was a native.

Throughout President Bush's later career—his vice presidency under Reagan, his four years in office, and his life after the presidency—I wanted to meet him. Not because I was particularly passionate about politics, or like to chase celebrities. My interest is from the historical perspective. I love history. And no one represents more history than a president.

Growing up just outside Detroit, I did manage to see Richard Nixon when he was running for president in 1968. Our ninth grade class had a field trip to a cavernous old hall in suburban Detroit to take part in a rally for the candidate. It was predictably colorful and definitely exciting, although I don't recall anything memorable about his speech. Plus, he wasn't the president at the time so he doesn't qualify.

I also shook Jimmy Carter's hand during his run for the office back in 1976. I was a student at the University of South Florida in Tampa. He appeared at a bandshell in town to speak. He passed my way after his address and turned to offer his hand. His grip and his greeting were friendly. Still, he hadn't yet been president, so he too doesn't qualify.

After four decades of sharing the same small town, I've seen President and Mrs. Bush many times at Memorial Day parades, yard sales, local gatherings, and even at the video store where Mrs. Bush was seen wearing one red and one blue tennis shoe and just re-learning to drive her new small car. But a sighting of the president is one thing; getting the opportunity to shake his hand, meet his eye, and ask him many questions about daily life in the White

House is quite another. Still, as close as we were, we were galaxies apart, and it seemed unlikely that I would ever get the opportunity to chat with 41.

I used to imagine what it would be like when I finally did meet him. We'd discuss the major issues of his presidency, hobnob about the economy, share our frustrations with Middle East policy, recount the tense days leading up the Gulf War, and kick back and learn more about what he really felt like after his surprising loss to Clinton. I envisioned a network news-like discourse; a lively exchange of views and reviews fit for an article in the *Atlantic Monthly*. Alas, when the moment actually did arrive, it didn't quite live up to my expectations. Not that he was a disappointment; it's just that the subject matter wasn't quite what I expected.

Life is about connections, which is precisely how opportunity knocked on my door one day when a local friend— John Dickinson—asked if I was free to take a photograph of him and his sister presenting the president wth a product that John and his father had designed: a *Bird Beakin'* lighthouse bird feeder. Knowing that a famous face shown receiving a product is tantamount to an endorsement, John's father, the inventor of the *Bird Beakin'*, had called on his old friend to inquire if he would be willing to be photographed receiving the inaugural feeder. Remarkably enough, the president agreed. Hence, the doors to Walker's Point were indirectly thrown open for me.

At the appointed morning hour, John, his sister Jill, and I, with camera bag in tow, drove up the winding driveway to Walker's

Point where we were directed by the Secret Service agent in the guardhouse to a parking space hidden by high bushes. As we expected, a second agent greeted us as soon as we exited the car. He was pleasant enough, dressed casually in khakis, a golf shirt, and sporting the predictable wire in the ear.

I've never yet quite figured out why they call them the Secret Service. They're anything but. Try as they may, during the 12 years of the Bush vice presidency and presidency, his guardians were a dismal failure at blending in with the locals. Since they were probably guided in dress by a family more in tune with the Ivy League set than the working class fishing families, they stood out like Zulus at a Maine clambake. Even if they did manage to occasionally hit the right outfit, the sunglasses, ear wires, and jet black SUVs were a dead giveaway. Still,

the need was understood and the effort was appreciated as it gave the true locals plenty to talk about at the bean suppers.

With *Bird Beakin'* in hand, we were escorted to one of the three small shingled cottages at the front end of the property. The door opened to a rustic entry hall sheathed in cottage wood dark with age and bearing just a touch of the pleasant salt-musty smell of a hundred summers. In front of us a stairway rose to a second floor landing. The agent pointed up the stairs and, before leaving, said, "The president is waiting for you in his office upstairs. It's the door on the right."

John led the way, his footsteps launching a cacophony of wooden creaking, gasping and groaning as if the aged wooden steps were fussy old folks tired of hosting so many feet. The cottage and its smell reminded me of a recent visit to

Franklin Delano Roosevelt's Campobello cottage. Only this time the president was still in residence.

As John entered the open door at the top of the stairs, an oddly familiar voice called out a hearty greeting. "Hi John! How is your Dad and Mom?" John then turned and introduced his sister and me as we rounded the corner into the room. Although I had seen the president from a distance several times over the years, up close I was surprised by his height. He was much taller than I expected, although his voice had the familiar reedy tone heard frequently on TV and radio over the previous years.

The office looked like a Maine cottage interpretation of the Oval Office. The main desk was a large, wooden antique surrounded by old ship models, memorabilia, and an American flag, which seemed appropriate, even if its presence would have been considered unusual in a similar setting at the neighbor's house.

The president was dressed casually, with a neatly pressed blue jean workshirt and khaki pants. His black hair, with its flecks of gray, seemed more shoved aside than combed, like a man enjoying a newly rediscovered ability to relax. He was cheerful and welcoming, and spent several minutes catching up on any local news John could share. I'm sure that he was still smarting from losing his re-election bid only months before. Still, my general impression was one of warmth and sincerity. I may have been mislead by a well-practiced politician, but darned if he didn't seem genuinely pleased to see us!

141

After discussing a boat model or two that had caught John's eye, John and Jill sat down with the former leader of the free world to discuss, of all things, birds. I pulled out the camera and began firing away.

For the next 30 minutes, the president and his guests talked about the bird feeder as if it was the most important thing on earth.

"You know, John, I've seen some of the most beautiful birds out here on Walker's Point."

"Absolutely, Mr. President," replied John sincerely. "And you know this *Bird Beakin'* will draw 'em like flies."

Quickly dismantling the sample, John launched into an impromptou sales patter. "My Dad designed the top to be easily removed so you can refill the base without spilling bird seed everywhere."

Next John pointed to a little metal rod protruding from the side of the lighthouse. It was coated with a black rubberized material. "And the little perch is wrapped in a special covering that improves grip," he emphasized with a grand gesture.

This point seemed to especially impress the president, who raised one eyebrow before looking over the feeder with the discerning eye of someone who takes bird feeders very seriously.

I circled behind John, to the side of Jill, around the edge of the desk, and all the way to the back of the room, getting as many angles as I could, as fast as possible, thinking all the time

that the discussion would run a few brief moments before petering out. I fired through a few rolls of film before I realized that this wasn't going to be the case.

"Did you know that in the Rose Garden I used to see a wonderful variety of birds?"

"I bet," countered John. "We get a lot of species up here in the summer, especially in the spring when they're all heading north for the season. You probably get quite a variety of birds here on Walker's Point."

And so it went, my big moment with the president, and all I can do is listen to a discussion about birds and their feeding habits.

Finally the time came to wrap it up. After reaching in a side drawer and presenting each of us with a presidential seal tie clasp, President Bush escorted us out the door and on to the lawn where I managed to grab some additional shots, including the official presentation of the first *Bird Beakin'*.

Recognizing an opportunity, I dropped the camera in John's hands and asked the president if he would mind taking a picture with me. He politely agreed. We sidled up together, grasped hands and smiled toward the lens as if we were long lost members of Yale's Whiffenpoof Society; the president's father, Prescott, actually had been a member. John caught the moment on film.

My meeting with the president may not have been the summit I dreamed about but it did have some good results. The photo of the three *Bird Beakin'* fans

appeared in local publications and sales were brisk. The president went on to help his son get elected (perhaps helped locally by his bird feeder photo in the town newspapers). The *Bird Beakin'* bird feeders appeared in stores throughout New England, even though John's father eventually sold the business.

I never did get the answers to all my questions about daily life in the White House or dramatic insights into the making of momentous decisions. Still, it gave me the opportunity to meet the former President of the United States. And despite the fact that his seasonal presence in Kennebunkport is considered routine by the locals, and many other folks have a more active relationship with the Bush family, individually it was a historic moment for me, even though the entire focus of the visit was, quite literally, for the birds.

Tim Dietz

FOR A GOOD CAUSE

143

From left: New England Patriots quarterback Tom Brady, President Bill Clinton, President Bush, and CBS Sportscaster Jim Nantz were a formidable foursome at one of the George H.W. Bush Celebrity Classic tournaments.

The generosity of President and Mrs. Bush to so many national and high profile causes is no secret. However, their immediate response to the local story of Gary Pike of Kennebunk and the hardship and distress endured by his mother in dealing with Gary's cancer diagnosis is lesser known. Gary was a life-long Kennebunk resident who died in 1991 at a very young age from a rare form of cancer. During his treatments, Gary and his family experienced first hand the financial hardship and stress families experience while staying away from home. When the community came together to support Gary and his family, President Bush also stepped forward to offer support for the Pike family and many others in similar situations.

For more than two decades, the president helped raise millions of dollars to support a stately, nine-bedroom home in Portland, Maine, known as Gary's House, to ensure that families in similar situations had an affordable place to stay while keeping watch or standing by when a sudden health care crisis required a lengthy hospitalization or long-term treatments.

Gary's House is operated by Northern Light Mercy Hospital in Portland, about 25 miles north of Kennebunkport, for the benefit of families with loved ones undergoing medical care at any hospital in southern Maine. Operations are fully funded by private gifts and an annual golf tournament—the George H.W. Bush Celebrity Classic for Gary's House—held at Cape Arundel Golf Club in Kennebunkport. It is one of only two tournaments in the country with

Kennebunkport resident Tom Norton serves as auctioneer for one of the George H.W. Bush Celebrity Classic for Gary's House events as Mrs. Bush joins in the fun at the Shawmut Inn in Kennebunkport.

the distinction of being named in the president's honor. Indeed, many of those associated with this tournament have been involved for years and, in many ways, each June event is something of a reunion for the volunteers and golf participants. It's not unusual for weekend guests at Walker's Point to make surprise appearances and even form a golf foursome, including President Bill Clinton, President George W. Bush, and best-selling author Jon Meacham. Other celebrities, such as CBS sportscaster Jim Nantz, former Red Sox all-star Luis Tiant, and New England Patriots quarterback Tom Brady, supported the cause based on the president's example and/or his hard-to-refuse personal invitation to join in the fun.

An evening auction following the tournament seemed to be especially fun for the 41st President. He was quick to offer anything of personal value to help support the fundraising. When he learned that the theme of the event one year was "Mission Impossible," his briefcase arrived as a donation. In other years, he sent his favorite putter, and even his signed golf bag. The list was impressive and drew thousands of dollars in bids. One had the impression that he walked

around the Point looking for items to support the auction. Case in point: When renowned presidential dog *Millie* gave birth to a litter of new springer spaniels, a new puppy was added as a part of the live auction.

His delight in hearing how much was raised each year was infectious. When he learned that a special "Presidents' Club"—a group with 41 members—was being formed to support the event, he was equally pleased. When Mrs. Bush learned of the Club, she proclaimed, "I think I need to be a part of that, too."

If you have the opportunity to visit Gary's House at 97 State Street in Portland, you will see the handiwork and in-kind donations of many Kennebunkport residents who got involved because of their love for President and Mrs. Bush. One of the most notable items is a portrait of Robin Bush, their lovely daughter whom they lost to cancer, that hangs in the living room.

The story of Gary Pike struck a chord in President and Mrs. Bush. True to form, they opened their hearts and the community followed.

Susan Rouillard

145

FAITH

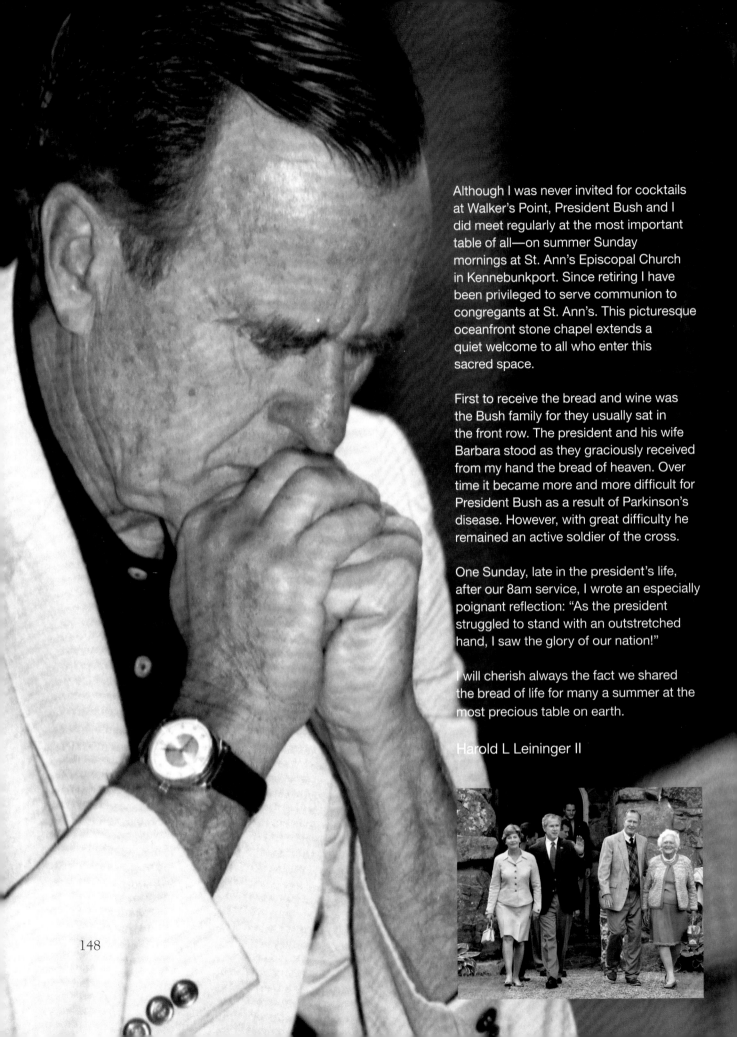

Although I was never invited for cocktails at Walker's Point, President Bush and I did meet regularly at the most important table of all—on summer Sunday mornings at St. Ann's Episcopal Church in Kennebunkport. Since retiring I have been privileged to serve communion to congregants at St. Ann's. This picturesque oceanfront stone chapel extends a quiet welcome to all who enter this sacred space.

First to receive the bread and wine was the Bush family for they usually sat in the front row. The president and his wife Barbara stood as they graciously received from my hand the bread of heaven. Over time it became more and more difficult for President Bush as a result of Parkinson's disease. However, with great difficulty he remained an active soldier of the cross.

One Sunday, late in the president's life, after our 8am service, I wrote an especially poignant reflection: "As the president struggled to stand with an outstretched hand, I saw the glory of our nation!"

I will cherish always the fact we shared the bread of life for many a summer at the most precious table on earth.

Harold L Leininger II

My wife Patty and I arrived at the rectory of St. Ann's Episcopal Church in Kennebunkport one afternoon in June of 1992 to begin 22 years of chaplaincy. The Vestry Council of St. Ann's was having a meeting in the rectory. The Most Reverend John M. Allin, retired Bishop of Mississippi and retired Presiding Bishop of the Episcopal Church, was conducting the meeting. As I entered the room, President Bush immediately stood and walked toward me to welcome me there. How honored I was to be greeted initially by him. George Herbert Walker Bush welcomed all people because that was the kind of gentleman he was. We initiated a Fourth of July service at the outdoor chapel and President Bush often read the lessons and served the Sacrament of Holy Communion. I could see and hear him enjoying the patriotic hymns of our service. I am honored and grateful to have been in his company.

The Very Reverend M.L. Agnew, Jr.

149

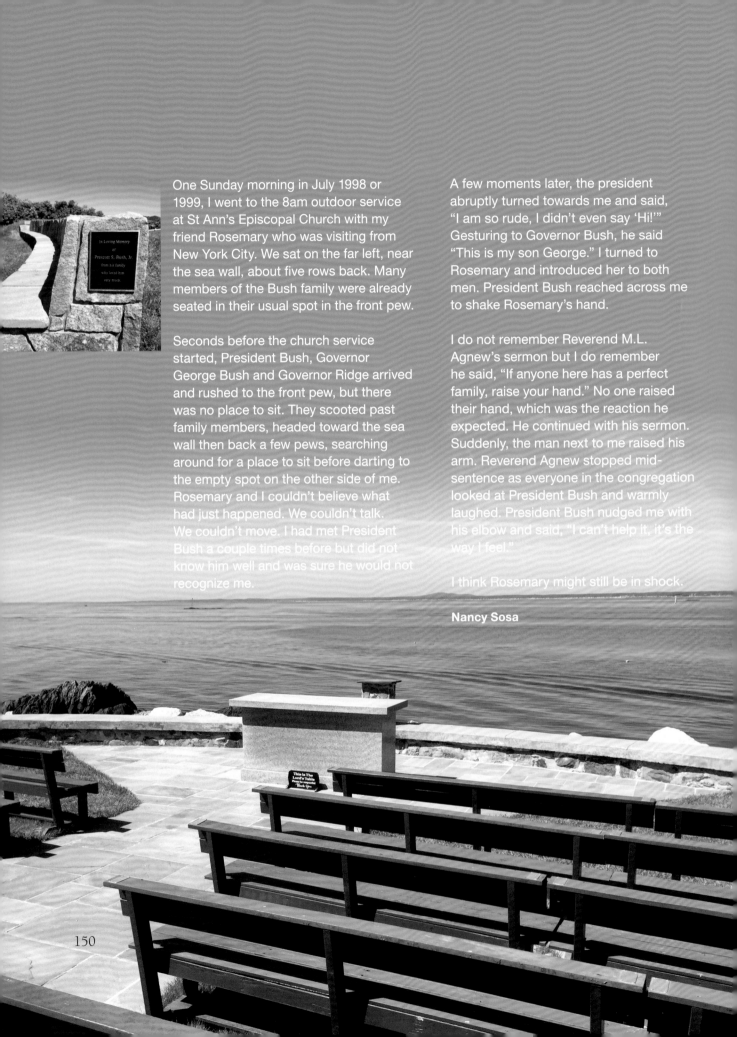

One Sunday morning in July 1998 or 1999, I went to the 8am outdoor service at St Ann's Episcopal Church with my friend Rosemary who was visiting from New York City. We sat on the far left, near the sea wall, about five rows back. Many members of the Bush family were already seated in their usual spot in the front pew.

Seconds before the church service started, President Bush, Governor George Bush and Governor Ridge arrived and rushed to the front pew, but there was no place to sit. They scooted past family members, headed toward the sea wall then back a few pews, searching around for a place to sit before darting to the empty spot on the other side of me. Rosemary and I couldn't believe what had just happened. We couldn't talk. We couldn't move. I had met President Bush a couple times before but did not know him well and was sure he would not recognize me.

A few moments later, the president abruptly turned towards me and said, "I am so rude, I didn't even say 'Hi!'" Gesturing to Governor Bush, he said "This is my son George." I turned to Rosemary and introduced her to both men. President Bush reached across me to shake Rosemary's hand.

I do not remember Reverend M.L. Agnew's sermon but I do remember he said, "If anyone here has a perfect family, raise your hand." No one raised their hand, which was the reaction he expected. He continued with his sermon. Suddenly, the man next to me raised his arm. Reverend Agnew stopped mid-sentence as everyone in the congregation looked at President Bush and warmly laughed. President Bush nudged me with his elbow and said, "I can't help it, it's the way I feel."

I think Rosemary might still be in shock.

Nancy Sosa

150

President and Mrs. Barbara Bush worshipped at Church on the Cape in Cape Porpoise for many years when St. Ann's Episcopal Church, their traditional place of worship, was not open for Sunday service in the offseason. One Memorial Day, after the Sunday service concluded, the congregation at Church on the Cape chose to raise the U.S. flag in a brief ceremony to commemorate those who died in prior wars. All the congregants gathered around the flagpole with President and Mrs. Bush and, in this case, with their daughter Doro on hand. It was a proud moment for all of us as the former president led in the salute to fallen heroes on a beautiful Memorial Day. He was a true patriot.

Rob Olson
US Navy '67-'71

President Bush and I shared the same birthday. At the First Parish Church service in Kennebunkport we always joked about who was the oldest, him or me.

Norma Little

President and Mrs. Bush would occasionally come to services at the First Congregational Church in Kennebunkport. They both were very warm and welcoming individuals who were gracious about allowing those in attendance to take photos with them.

Samantha Gerry

151

When death comes, as it does to us all, life is changed, not ended—and the way we live our lives, the decisions we make, the service we render—matter. They matter to our fellow humans, to this world God has given to us, and to God.

Few people have understood this as well as President George H. W. Bush. It was as natural to him as breathing is to each of us. President Bush was a good man; he was a godly man, full of grace, love and a quality absolutely necessary to enter the kingdom of God—humility, grounded in a desire to serve His God and all God sent His way.

How do I know this? Because for nearly a dozen years, my wife, Laura, and our children have laughed and fished with him. President George W. Bush mentioned how much his father enjoyed going full throttle on *Fidelity*. We have had that pleasure with the 41st President. One time, we were out in *Fidelity* with the Secret Service following close behind. We saw them reaching into their coats for what I thought might have been some form of protection—it was only then we realized they were crossing themselves!

We have been blessed to share meals, tears, moments of silence, and prayers in times of great strength and in times of great weakness. Never did I witness anything but care for those around him.

Our lesson from the Hebrew Scriptures remind us that God is Light—and the president reflected that light his whole life through. He once said, "I am a man who sees life in terms of missions defined and missions completed." We recall with delight when he reminded America of

his mission and ours—to be "points of light," with but one aim: to leave our world better than we found it.

I have a political cartoon of 41 with caricatured big ears and glasses. He's at his desk, looking at his watch and saying to himself: "Communism is dead, the wall is down, apartheid is falling, Mandela is free, the Sandinistas are ousted, Germany is reuniting, the Cold War is over, I've returned my calls, and heck, it's not even lunchtime."

We sometimes forget all President Bush did for us, in large part because he preferred to shine, not to be shined upon. Several years ago, President Bush gave me a plaque. It read "Preach Christ at all times…if necessary, use words." It remains on my desk as a reminder that faith means more than words. Jesus Christ, for George Bush, was at the heart of his faith—but his was a deep faith, a generous faith, a simple faith, in the best sense of the word. He knew and lived Jesus' two greatest commandments—to love God, and love your neighbor. The president loved and served not just some, but all God sent his way. He lived his own adage—"Tolerance is a virtue, not a vice." He respected and befriended Christians of every denomination as well as Jews, Muslims, Buddhists, and Sikhs. His comrades were from every nation and race. Yes, he was a Republican, but for him political parties were but a line in the sand to brush away in the times of the greater good of working toward his goal for all of us to be a "kinder and gentler nation."

Recently, I was humbled, along with the loving members of the president's family and his wonderful medical aides, to be at the president's side at his passing. Also present was someone that the president liked to call his "little brother": James Baker and his wife Susan. There had been wonderful and kind words and hugs and kisses through the day. Toward the end, Secretary Baker pointed at the president, and whispered, "You know, that man changed my life."

I have been at the deathbed of many people over the years, but what followed is something I will never forget. A bit later, Secretary Baker was at the foot of the president's bed. Jim rubbed and stroked the president's feet for perhaps half an hour. The president smiled at this comfort from his dear friend. Here I witnessed a world leader who was serving; and a servant who had been our world's leader. What came to mind was Jesus. On that last night before His own crucifixion, having said everything there was to say, He wrapped a towel around His waist and without words—He washed His disciples feet. As Jesus finished, He said: "I have set an example for you. Do as I have done. Serve one another. By this the world will know you are my disciples—if you love one another."

At the end, we all knelt, placed our hands on the president, and said our prayers together. And then we were silent, as this man—who had changed all of our lives, our nation, and our world, left this life for the next.

For a moment, but a moment only, that dear point of Light we know as George Herbert Walker Bush dimmed, but now it shines, brighter than ever.

And now, this godly man, this servant, this child of God is in the loving arms of his Barbara and Robin and the welcoming arms of our Lord, who embraced him with His divine love.

The president so loved our great country. He loved his Church—the Episcopal Church. He loved you—his friends—and he loved every single member of his family. But he was so ready to go to heaven...and heaven was so ready to receive him because he lived those great two commandments.

If you want to honor this man—if you call yourself a daughter or son of God—then love one another. Serve and love one another. There is no greater mission than these.

My hunch is heaven, as perfect as it must be, just got a bit kinder and gentler, leaving behind a hole for you and me to fill. How? Preach Christ at all times. If necessary, use words.

So, Mr. President, mission complete. Well done good and faithful servant. Welcome to your eternal home where the ceiling and visibility are unlimited and where they go on forever.

The Reverend Dr. Russell J. Levenson, Jr.

155

FAREWELL

I once heard it said of man that the idea is to die young as late as possible.

At age 85, a favorite pastime of George H.W. Bush was firing up his boat, *Fidelity*, and opening up the three 300 horsepower engines to fly, joyfully fly across the Atlantic with the Secret Service boats straining to keep up.

At age 90, George H.W. Bush parachuted out of an aircraft and landed on the grounds of St. Ann's by the Sea in Kennebunkport, the church where his mom was married and where he worshipped often. Mother liked to say he chose the location just in case the chute didn't open.

In his 90s, he took great delight when his closest pal, James A. Baker, smuggled a bottle of *Grey Goose* vodka into his hospital room. Apparently it paired well with the steak Baker had delivered from Morton's.

To his very last days, Dad's life was instructive. As he aged he taught us how to grow with dignity, humor and kindness. When the good Lord finally called, he knew how to meet him with courage and with the joy of the promise of what lies ahead.

One reason Dad knew how to die young is that he almost did it, twice. When he was a teenager, a staph infection nearly took his life. A few years later he was alone in the Pacific on a life raft, praying that his rescuers would find him before the enemy did. God answered those prayers. It turned out he had other plans for George H.W. Bush.

For Dad's part, I think those brushes with death made him cherish the gift of life, and he vowed to live every day to the fullest.

Dad was always busy, a man in constant motion, but never too busy to share his love of life with those around him. He taught us to love the outdoors. He loved watching dogs flush a covey. He loved landing the illusive striper. And once confined to a wheelchair, he seemed happiest sitting in his favorite perch on the back porch at Walker's Point contemplating the majesty of the Atlantic.

The horizons he saw were bright and hopeful. He was a genuinely optimistic man, and that optimism guided his

> **To his very last days, Dad's life was instructive. As he aged he taught us how to grow with dignity, humor and kindness.**

children and made each of us believe that anything was possible. He continually broadened his horizons with daring decisions.

He was a patriot. After high school he put college on hold and became a navy fighter pilot as World War II broke out.

Like many of his generation, he never talked about his service until his time as a public figure forced his hand. We learned of the attack on Chichi Jima, the mission completed, the shoot down. We learned of the death of his crewmates whom he thought about throughout his entire life. And we learned of the rescue.

And then another audacious decision; he moved his young family from the comforts of the East coast to Odessa, Texas. He and Mom adjusted to their arid surroundings quickly. He was a tolerant man. After all, he was kind and neighborly

to the women with whom he, Mom and I shared a bathroom in our small duplex. Even after he learned of their profession, ladies of the night.

Dad could relate to people from all walks of life. He was an empathetic man. He valued character over pedigree, and he was no cynic. He looked for the good in each person and he usually found it.

Dad taught us that public service is noble and necessary, that one can serve with integrity and hold true to the important values like faith and family. He strongly believed that it was important to give back to the community and country in which one lived. He recognized that serving others enriched the giver's soul. To us, his was the brightest of a thousand points of light.

In victory he shared credit. When he lost, he shouldered the blame. He accepted

On e-mail he had a circle of friends with whom he shared or received the latest jokes. His grading system for the quality of the joke was classic George Bush. The rare 7s and 8s were considered huge winners, most of them off-color.

George Bush knew how to be a true and loyal friend. He nurtured and honored his many friendships with a generous and giving soul. There exists thousands of handwritten notes encouraging or sympathizing or thanking his friends and acquaintances.

He had an enormous capacity to give of himself. Many a person would tell you that Dad became a mentor and a father figure in their life. He listened and he consoled. He was their friend. I think of Don Rhodes, Taylor Blanton, Jim Nantz, Arnold Schwarzenegger, and perhaps the unlikeliest of all, the man who defeated him, Bill Clinton. My siblings and I refer to the guys in this group as brothers from other mothers.

He taught us that a day was not meant to be wasted. He played golf at a legendary pace. I always wonder why he insisted on

that failure is a part of living a full life, but taught us never to be defined by failure. He showed us how setbacks can strengthen.

None of his disappointments could compare with one of life's greatest tragedies, the loss of a young child.

Jeb and I were too young to remember the pain and agony he and Mom felt when our 3-year-old sister died. We only learned later that Dad, a man of quiet faith, prayed for her daily. He was sustained by the love of the Almighty and the real and enduring love of her Mom. Dad always believed that one day he would hug his precious Robin again.

He loved to laugh, especially at himself. He could tease and needle but never out of malice. He placed great value on a good joke. That's why he chose (Senator Alan) Simpson to speak.

160

speed golf; he's a good golfer. Here's my conclusion. He played fast so he could move on to the next event, to enjoy the rest of the day, to expend his enormous energy, to live it all. He was born with just two settings, full throttle, then sleep. He taught us what it means to be a wonderful father, grandfather and great grandfather. He was firm in his principles and supportive as we began to seek our own ways. He encouraged and comforted but never steered. We tested his patience. I know I did. But he always responded with the great gift of unconditional love. Last Friday when I was told he had minutes to live, I called him. The guy answered the phone, said "I think he can hear you but he hasn't said anything for most of the day." I said, "Dad, I love you and you've been a wonderful father," and the last words he would ever say on Earth were, "I love you too."

To us he was close to perfect, but not totally. His short game was lousy. He wasn't exactly Fred Astaire on the dance floor. The man couldn't stomach vegetables, especially broccoli. And by the way, he passed these genetic defects along to us.

Finally, every day of his 73 years of marriage, Dad taught us all what it means to be a great husband. He married his sweetheart. He adored her. He laughed and cried with her. He was dedicated to her totally.

In his old age Dad enjoyed watching police show reruns, the volume on high, all the while holding Mom's hand. After Mom died, Dad was strong, but all he really wanted to do was hold Mom's hand again.

Of course Dad taught me another special lesson. He showed me what it means to be a president who serves with integrity, leads with courage and acts with love in his heart for the citizens of our country.

When the history books are written, they will say that George H.W. Bush was a great President of the United

States, a diplomat of unmatched skill, a Commander in Chief of formidable accomplishment, and a gentleman who executed the duties of his office with dignity and honor.

In his inaugural address the 41st President of the United States said this: "We cannot hope only to leave our children a bigger car, a bigger bank account, we must hope to give them a sense of what it means to be a loyal friend, a loving parent, a citizen who leaves his home, his neighborhood and town better than he found it. What do we want the men and women who work with us to say when we are no longer there? That we were more driven to succeed than anyone around us or that we stopped to ask if a sick child had gotten better and stayed a moment there to trade a word of friendship?"

Well, Dad, we're going to remember you for exactly that and much more, and we're going to miss you. Your decency, sincerity, and kind soul will stay with us forever. So through our tears, let us know the blessings of knowing and loving you, a great and noble man. The best father a son or daughter could have. And in our grief, let us smile knowing that Dad is hugging Robin and holding Mom's hand again.

PRESIDENTIAL HISTORIAN JON MEACHAM, who wrote a best-selling biography of former President George H.W. Bush, was one of four people chosen to eulogize Mr. Bush at his funeral at the National Cathedral in Washington, D.C. Here is a transcript of his remarks:

The story was almost over even before it had fully begun. Shortly after dawn on Saturday, September 2, 1944, Lieutenant Junior Grade George Herbert Walker Bush joined by two crewmates took off from the USS San Jacinto to attack a radio tower on Chichi Jima. As they approached the target, the air was heavy with flack. The plane was hit. Smoke filled the cockpit. Flames raced across the wings. "My God," Lieutenant Bush thought, "This thing's going to go down." Yet he kept the plane in its 35-degree dive, dropped his bombs, and then roared off out to sea telling his crewmates to hit the silk.

Following protocol, Lieutenant Bush turned the plane so they could bail out. Only then did Bush parachute from the cockpit. The wind propelled him backward and he gashed his head on the tail of the plane as he flew through the sky. He plunged deep into the ocean, bobbed to the surface, and flopped onto a tiny raft. His head bleeding, his eyes burning, his mouth and throat raw from saltwater, the future 41st President of the United States was alone. Sensing that his men had not made it, he was overcome. He felt the weight of responsibility as a nearly physical burden and he wept.

Then, at four minutes shy of noon, a submarine emerged to rescue the downed pilot. George Herbert Walker Bush was safe. The story, his story and ours, would go on by God's grace. Through the ensuing decades, President Bush would frequently ask, nearly daily, he'd ask himself why me? Why was I spared? And in a sense, the rest of his life was a perennial effort to prove himself worthy of his salvation on that distant morning.

To him, his life was no longer his own. There were always more missions to undertake more lives to touch, and more love to give. And what a headlong race he made of it all. He never slowed down. On the primary campaign trail in New Hampshire once, he grabbed the hand of a department store mannequin asking for votes.

When he realized his mistake, he said, "Never know. Got to ask." You can hear the voice, can't you? As Dana Carvey said, the key to a Bush 41 impersonation is Mr. Rogers trying to be John Wayne.

George Herbert Walker Bush was America's last great soldier statesman, a 20th-century founding father. He governed with virtues that most closely resembled those of Washington and of Adams, of TR and of FDR, of Truman and Eisenhower, of men who believed in causes larger than themselves. Six foot two, handsome, dominant in person, President Bush spoke with those big strong hands making fists to underscore points.

A master of what Franklin Roosevelt called the science of human relationships, he believed that to whom much is given, much is expected. And because life gave him so much, he gave back again and again and again. He stood in the breach

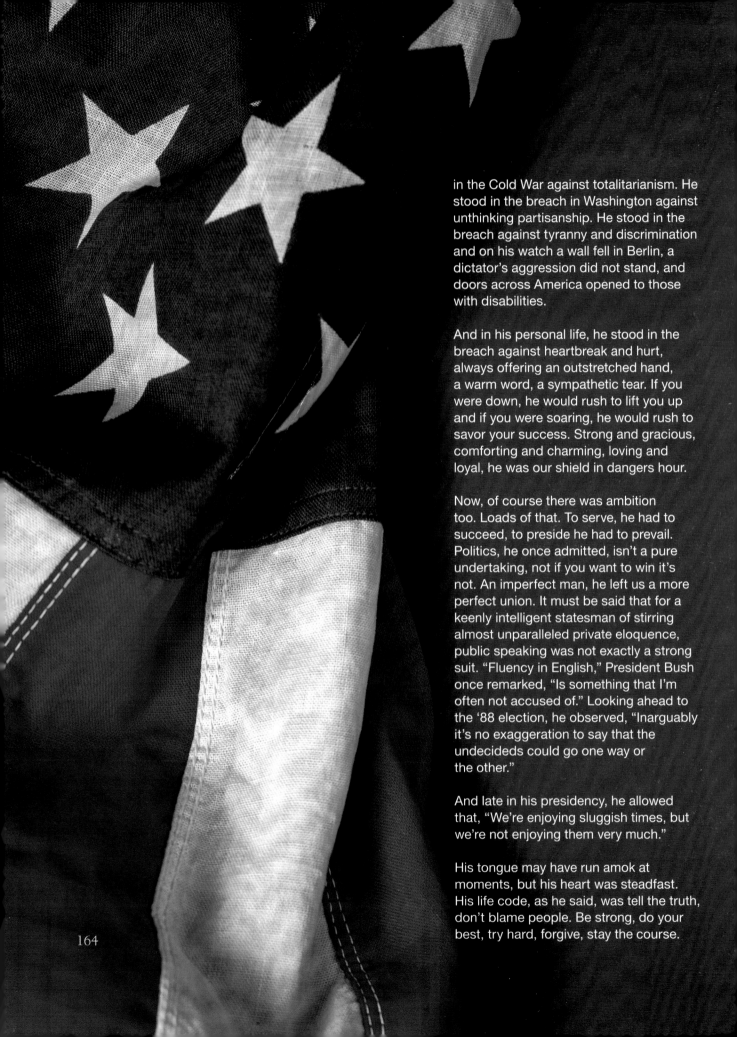

in the Cold War against totalitarianism. He stood in the breach in Washington against unthinking partisanship. He stood in the breach against tyranny and discrimination and on his watch a wall fell in Berlin, a dictator's aggression did not stand, and doors across America opened to those with disabilities.

And in his personal life, he stood in the breach against heartbreak and hurt, always offering an outstretched hand, a warm word, a sympathetic tear. If you were down, he would rush to lift you up and if you were soaring, he would rush to savor your success. Strong and gracious, comforting and charming, loving and loyal, he was our shield in dangers hour.

Now, of course there was ambition too. Loads of that. To serve, he had to succeed, to preside he had to prevail. Politics, he once admitted, isn't a pure undertaking, not if you want to win it's not. An imperfect man, he left us a more perfect union. It must be said that for a keenly intelligent statesman of stirring almost unparalleled private eloquence, public speaking was not exactly a strong suit. "Fluency in English," President Bush once remarked, "Is something that I'm often not accused of." Looking ahead to the '88 election, he observed, "Inarguably it's no exaggeration to say that the undecideds could go one way or the other."

And late in his presidency, he allowed that, "We're enjoying sluggish times, but we're not enjoying them very much."

His tongue may have run amok at moments, but his heart was steadfast. His life code, as he said, was tell the truth, don't blame people. Be strong, do your best, try hard, forgive, stay the course.

And that was and is the most American of creeds. Abraham Lincoln's Better Angels of Our Nature and George H.W. Bush's Thousand Points of Light are companion verses in America's national hymn, for Lincoln and Bush both called on us to choose the right over the convenient, to hope rather than to fear, and to heed not our worst impulses, but our best instincts.

In this work, he had the most wonderful of allies in Barbara Pierce Bush, his wife of 73 years. He called her Barb, the silver fox, and when the situation warranted, the enforcer. He was the only boy she ever kissed. Her children, Mrs. Bush liked to say, always wanted to throw up when they heard that. In a letter to Barbara during the war, young George H.W. Bush had written, "I love you, precious, with all my heart and to know that you love me means my life. How lucky our children will be to have a mother like you." And as they will tell you, they surely were.

As Vice President, Bush once visited a children's leukemia ward in Krakow. 35 years before, he and Barbara had lost a daughter, Robin, to the disease. In Krakow, a small boy wanted to greet the American vice president. Learning that the child was sick with the cancer that had taken Robin, Bush began to cry. To his diary later that day, the vice president said this. "My eyes flooded with tears and behind me was a bank of television cameras and I thought I can't turn around. I can't dissolve because of personal tragedy in the face of the nurses that give of themselves every day. So I stood there looking at this little guy tears running down my cheek hoping he wouldn't see. But if he did, hoping he'd feel that I loved him."

That was the real George H.W. Bush,

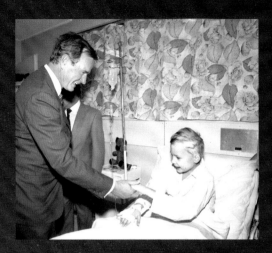

a loving man with a big, vibrant, all-enveloping heart. And so we ask as we commend his soul to God, and has he did, why him? Why was he spared? The workings of Providence are mysterious but this much is clear, that George Herbert Walker Bush, who survived that fiery fall into the waters of the Pacific three quarters of a century ago, made our lives and the lives of nations freer, better, warmer, and nobler. That was his mission. That was his heartbeat. And if we listen closely enough, we can hear that heartbeat even now, for it's the heartbeat of a lion, a lion who not only led us, but who loved us. That's why him. That's why he was spared.

First published on December 6, 2018

Jon Meacham

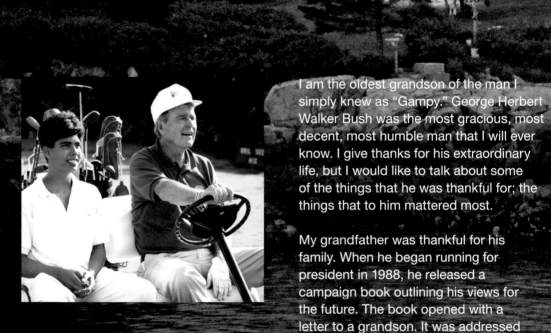

I am the oldest grandson of the man I simply knew as "Gampy." George Herbert Walker Bush was the most gracious, most decent, most humble man that I will ever know. I give thanks for his extraordinary life, but I would like to talk about some of the things that he was thankful for; the things that to him mattered most.

My grandfather was thankful for his family. When he began running for president in 1988, he released a campaign book outlining his views for the future. The book opened with a letter to a grandson. It was addressed to me and recounted some of our recent experiences together in Maine.

"P.," the letter read, "I have been thinking about it a lot. The most fun was the big rock boat, climbing out on it, and watching you playing on it. Near the end of summer when the moon was full, the

tides were high, there was that special day when it almost seemed like the boat was real."

In those few words, my grandfather said more about his life than I could ever tell you this morning. Here's a man gearing up for the role of a lifetime, and yet his mind went back to his family. This is a book about policy issues, and yet he still found time to write about an imaginary boat that he built with his grandson. And in a typical day, he would wake up around 5:00 a.m. to review security briefings and grab his first coffee of the day. And when the coast was clear, the grandkids would try to snag a spot on the bed and nestle up between him and Ganny when they read the paper. We all grew up in awe of my grandfather, who we would catch fly fishing off the rocks of Maine, talking up where the blue fish were running. He would be the first to host an intense horseshoe matchup among family, Secret Service, or any willing head of state, while encouraging trash talk like "power outage" if your horseshoe was short, or "Woodrow Wilson" if your toss was long and your shoe hit the wooden backstop.

His typical spread included barbecue, tacos, tamales, and pork rinds with hot sauce, with a healthy complement of Blue Bell ice cream and Klondike bars. Always the competitor, each night Gampy challenged all of the grandkids to the coveted "first to sleep" award. In classic Gampy fashion, he would write letters of encouragement to us all, whether one of us had a hard semester at school, whether one of us—and for the record, not me—drove his *Fidelity* onto the rocks, or one of us—definitely not me—ended up in Ganny's crosshairs. I knew too much.

George P. Bush

167

"Giving back is a great thing for someone to do Walker. When you are a bigger guy, you should consider it."

Dear Uncle George,

This is a tribute I actually hoped never to write. You were always someone I had hoped could live forever, though deep down I knew it impossible even for you.

On my son Craig's bedroom wall is the first letter you ever wrote to me or actually about me to my parents the day after I was born; April 16, 1974. In the letter you asked my parents to do you one favor, to please if they ever got sick of me to just leave me off with you so you could love and care for me. I had no idea then that my life for the next 44 years would be filled and enriched by your boundless capacity for love in more ways than I could ever have imagined.

Just down the stairs from Craig's room is a picture of one of my earliest memories, holding a stack of mackerel on the docks in Kennebunkport, Maine, after a fishing trip with you. I was six years old and you asked me to go fishing with you. I thought at the time this was the coolest thing in the world because I loved your fast boat. What I didn't know was that it was also the day after you were asked to be vice president. I remember coming back to the breakwater and seeing signs of love and support for you lining Maine's coastline. What's going on I think I asked and you replied "Giving back is a great thing for someone to do Walker. When you are a bigger guy, you should consider it." Kind of a hard day for me to ever forget Mr. President!

Over the years, I've collected dozens and dozens of personal letters from you about important matters like the family ranking committee for horseshoe and tennis tournaments.

There's a letter you wrote to me when a kid picked on me at school and another letter when I graduated from college. Your capacity to care about so many other people in life always astonished me. I remember how you attended the funeral and gave the eulogy for Woodrow Willoughby, the longtime elevator operator at the White House because he had become family. I remember getting the opportunity to ride with you to the Houston Astrodome to give your speech for re-election in 1992. Everyone in the room at the *Houstonian* was trying to rush you into the car to get you to your speech but you wouldn't budge. You wouldn't budge because the spouse of a staff member had cancer and you were too busy consoling the family. On one of the biggest nights of your life as president, you actually cared more about giving comfort to someone in need than anything else you could've or should've been doing that night.

"This is more important." I remember you saying through the door.

It is impossible for me to reflect on your vast life of service because it is simply too overwhelming that one person could accomplish so much in the one life we all share. Here, though, are a few small things I think everyone should know about you.

You were a man of deep faith who always managed to love your family first and always at just the right moment. Outside of family, your capacity for kindness and generosity to others knew no bounds. You were the most unfailingly gracious of men.

You carried yourself with deep humility and you told great stories. You had an incredible sense of humor and often it was self-deprecating. You always cared far more about people than politics. You had this incredible knack for making people around you feel special and important no matter if they were in the coatroom or at your dinner table. You have more friends than any man I'll ever know.

Mr. President, your deep and abiding love for our country and your lifetime of service is a testament to patriotism and heroism that will endure for the ages. You inspired me and thousands of others around the world to give something back to others through public service.

May our country never forget your legacy of service, sacrifice and selflessness.

Godspeed, and as you always loved to say, CAVU!

Walker Stapleton
Colorado Treasurer

We at the Kennebunkport Conservation Trust were deeply saddened by the passing of President George Herbert Walker Bush. He devoted his life to the service of his nation, from war hero to president, and like the nation, we will miss the sense of duty, honor and civility that he and his generation so admirably represented. We will miss the way that he would reach out to friend and foe alike in an effort to do what was best for the land as a whole. We will miss the wisdom he exhibited in knowing when to stand up for principle and when to step aside and let others shape a commonly desired future. We will miss his quiet voice and the steady course he tried to steer us towards a kinder and gentler nation.

Here in Kennebunkport, we will also miss him as a friend and a neighbor. This town, he was quick to point out, was his "anchor to windward", and he loved it in a way that was steeped in generations of family memories and traditions. This was where he could play and pray and tighten

the bonds of family and friends. As the waves rolled against the rocky shore by his seaside home, he could let his mind wander back to the countless happy days of his youth. Or, he could look into the eyes and hearts of his children and grandchildren and dream of what could be. It was where he gave and received love freely, a place where he could rekindle the fire within him for the many challenges he was destined to face.

We will miss his love for his wife, family, community and nation, his great good humor and fun-loving spirit, his generosity, competitive spirit, and inclusiveness. We will miss his decency. We will miss him. May God bless you Mr. President. You have served us well, and we are all enriched for having walked a bit of this path with you.

Tom Bradbury

171

173

174

Our friend, our neighbor, our hero.
We will carry you in our
hearts forever.

PHOTO CREDITS

Jean Becker
Susan Biddle
Tom Bradbury
George Bush Presidential Library and Museum
Robert Dennis
Tim Dietz
Tricia Gorman
The Goyette family
Ken Raynor
Lynn "Kip" Kippax
Bobby Koch
Cathy Koppstein
Lucy Muckerman Lamb
The Reverend Russell J. Levenson, Jr.
Norma Little
Peggy Liversidge
Johnny Morris
Rob Olson
Annie Kennedy Phelps
Susan Rouillard
Austin Sandler
Chris and Cyndi Smith, CA Smith Photography
Jeff Stevenson
The Tolley family
Meg Tower
Seacoast Media Group

If we have missed anyone who contributed a photograph to this publication, we apologize, as we tried to be as thorough as possible in recognizing contributors.

Special thanks to the crew at Dietz Associates Inc. in Kennebunk for their coordination and patience in the editing and design of this special publication. There were many stories and thousands of photographs that had to be sourced to make this happen. We are very grateful for their dedication in helping this book become a reality.

Proceeds from **Our President: Loving Memories of George H.W. Bush From His Friends in the Kennebunks** will be used to support the endowment for the Anchor To Windward, the monument on Ocean Avenue that overlooks Walker's Point, and Ganny's Garden, a garden in Kennebunkport created to honor and remember Barbara Bush. If you would like to contribute separately to the endowment, contributions can be sent to the Kennebunkport Conservation Trust, PO Box 7004, Cape Porpoise, ME 04014.